BECAUSE
OF THE
MESSIAH
IN A
MANGER

BECAUSE
OF THE
MESSIAH
IN A
MANGER

BRAD WILCOX

DESERET
BOOK

SALT LAKE CITY, UTAH

To my wonderful grandmother,
Mary Russell Camenish,
and all the Camenish cousins,
with whom some of my fondest
Christmas memories were made.

Library of Congress Cataloging-in-Publication Data
Names: Wilcox, Brad, author.
Title: Because of the Messiah in a manger / Brad Wilcox.
Description: Salt Lake City, Utah : Deseret Book, [2018] | Includes bibliographical references.
Identifiers: LCCN 2018018738 | ISBN 9781629724652 (paperbound)
Subjects: LCSH: Christmas. | Jesus Christ—Nativity. | Jesus Christ—Mormon interpretations. | The Church of Jesus Christ of Latter-day Saints—Doctrines. | Mormon Church—Doctrines.
Classification: LCC BX8643.J4 W55 2018 | DDC 263/.915—dc23
LC record available at https://lccn.loc.gov/2018018738

Printed in the United States of America
Lake Book Manufacturing, Inc., Melrose Park, IL

10   9   8   7   6   5   4   3   2   1

CONTENTS

Acknowledgments vii
Introduction ix

CHRIST AND HIS GIFTS

Light of the World 3
The Legend of the Poinsettia 11
The Trees of Christmas. 19

HOLY FAMILY

Son of the Blessed 27
Swaddling Clothes, Mangers, and Inns 32
Noel, Know Well. 38

SHEPHERDS AND ANGELS

The Good Shepherd 47
Feeding Lambs 53
Hearing the Angels' Songs. 62

WISE MEN

Recognizing the Star 73

Another Way 82

BELIEVERS WITHIN THE BOOK OF MORMON
AND AT JOSEPH SMITH'S TIME

A Gift Received 91

Seeing Christ More Clearly 97

DISCIPLES IN OUR DAY

Prophets Past, Present, and Future 105

Let's Get Christmasing! 113

Love Matters 122

Conclusion 131

"That Night in the Stable" 135

Notes 137

ACKNOWLEDGMENTS

When I speak to young children about the writing process, I remind them that writing is like playing basketball—it takes lots of shots and an entire team to win the game! I gratefully acknowledge the wonderful players on my team. Thanks to my wife, Debi, and my daughters, Wendee Rosborough and Whitney Laycock. I appreciate their careful editing and unfailing support and love. Thanks to all my family for experiencing with me so many of the stories I share in this book. You bring me joy at Christmas and all year.

Special thanks to Elder Craig A. Cardon, Jake Busby, Brett Sanders, Vicky Davenport, Jeanne Thompson, and Larry Laycock for allowing me to share insights I gleaned from them and to Janice Kapp Perry for generously granting permission for me to share a Christmas song she and my mother, Val C. Wilcox, wrote together.

I appreciate Lisa Roper at Deseret Book for sharing the idea for this Christmas book in the first place and for sticking with me from beginning to end. I also appreciate Sheri Dew, Laurel Christensen Day, Shauna Gibby, Tracy Keck, Malina Grigg, and Michelle Lippold at Deseret Book as well as Chrislyn Woolston, Tennisa Nordfelt, Laura Korth, and the rest of the Time Out for Women team. Dave Kimball and those who work with him in marketing are amazing. You are all the "trusted voices of light and knowledge" described in the Deseret Book mission statement.

INTRODUCTION

One December I saw a clever sign on the marquee of a Christian church: "Christmas is not *your* birthday!" I got their point, but I still had to disagree, because I was born right on December 25th. When I was younger, my parents were afraid my birthday would get overlooked in the holiday rush, so they made a big banner that hung in our home: "Happy Birthday to Jesus and Brad!" They also started a tradition of putting up two trees—one for Jesus and one for me. The idea was that my brothers had to put a present for me under each tree—a plan that worked well until my older brother bought me a pair of mittens. He placed one mitten under the Christmas tree and the other under the birthday tree, and everything went downhill from there. These days, most gifts just come with a "Merry Birthday" card to cover both occasions. Here's one I received from my cousin:

Being born on Christmas
Is quite unique because
You never know who brought you—
The stork or Santa Claus.

Despite the drawbacks, my Christmas birthday has always added sparkle to the season and made Christmas joyous. However, for some people, Christmas is not the happiest time of the year. Consider the parents waiting in line so their screaming children can see Santa. Think of the store employees who watch people stampede over each other like animals to get the latest electronic gadgets. What about the frazzled teachers who have to deal with children who have been loaded up on sugar since Halloween? Consider the delivery drivers who deal with furious customers when packages arrive late or the airport workers when flights are canceled.

In a more serious vein, Christmas is not always happy for those who are alone, are far from family, or have had a loved one die in a December past. I'm afraid the words "merry and bright" don't just automatically come with the season. They have to be a conscious choice.

I love teaching at Time Out for Women events. In some locations there is also a program called Time Out for Girls. Grandmas, aunts, moms, and Young Women leaders go out of their way to bring their teenage girls to listen to the music and speakers. First thing in the morning, the young women write questions on cards that presenters address later in the day. I enjoy reading those questions. I can really see the difference in the ages and maturity levels of the girls. One young woman wrote, "Do you ever get a headache thinking about the Creation and how there is no end to space and how matter cannot be created or destroyed?" The very next question was, "How do you feel about chicken nuggets?"

At one event in Portland, a young woman asked a question that has stuck with me. She wrote, "If this is called the plan of happiness, then why am I so miserable? #Falseadvertising." She's not the only one who has asked such a question when the realities of life have hit hard. Some face bullying and abuse. Others deal with physical, emotional, and mental health issues. There are those who struggle because of the poor choices of those around them, while others face consequences of their own bad decisions. Low self-esteem is compounded by poor communication skills and inability to deal effectively with pressure and stress. Add weak spirituality to that, and pretty soon we all end up wondering whether the plan of happiness is indeed false advertising.

Just as I did at that Time Out for Girls event, I

testify that it is not. Latter-day Saints are unique among Christians because we understand that God did not create the world with the goal for us all to live forever in the Garden of Eden. Mortality was Plan A, not Plan B. The Atonement of Christ was not a last-ditch attempt to salvage the wreckage Adam and Eve had made of the world. It was planned from the beginning (see Mosiah 4:6). Repentance was not provided as a safety net for those weak souls who could not be perfectly obedient. It was designed as an essential part of the perfecting process for each one of us.

> *God made suffering a required course in life, but growth had to be an elective.*

Mortality was meant to be a school—complete with hard teachers and difficult tests. God gave us freedom knowing full well it would lead to some bad choices. But freedom also offered the opportunity for learning. God made suffering a required course in life, but growth had to be an elective.

God's plan is called the plan of happiness not because everything is perfectly happy but because it is how we are happily perfected. In 2 Nephi we read, "Men are, that they might have joy" (2:25). In the footnote to that verse we read, "Potential to become like Heavenly Father."

President Russell M. Nelson has taught, "When the focus of our lives is on God's plan of salvation . . . and Jesus Christ and His gospel, we can feel joy regardless of what is happening—or not happening—in our lives. Joy comes from and because of Him. He is the source of all joy. We feel it at Christmastime when we sing, 'Joy to the world, the Lord is come' (*Hymns*, no. 201). And we can feel it all year round. For Latter-day Saints, Jesus Christ is joy!"[1]

> *Christ did not perform the Atonement to free us from suffering but to be able to be with us in our suffering.*

Christ did not perform the Atonement to free us from suffering but to be able to be with us in our suffering. The goal was that we would be comforted, not comfortable. Progress and growth are seldom comfortable, but they are always worth it. The Atonement of Christ is not only about overcoming death and sin. The Lord also carried our pains, sicknesses, mistakes, and heartaches. Because He descended below them all, He can offer consolation and comfort during challenges, perspective and peace during trials, and divine assistance through it all.

When one young missionary I will call Elder Baker entered the MTC, his family was strong and united—at least that is what he thought. About halfway through his mission his mother shocked everyone by filing for a divorce. After twenty-five years of what Elder Baker had believed was a solid temple marriage, everything came unglued. He heard the news from his mission president, who had received a call from Elder Baker's father. So many questions filled this young man's mind, and no one had answers: Where were his folks now? What about his siblings? Were they still going to church? What did this mean for the future? Why had he not seen this coming? Why had his parents kept this from him?

Deep down, there were other questions—crazy questions Elder Baker didn't even want to admit he had: Was this somehow his fault? Had he not been a good enough son? Where was God? Was this how God blessed him for his missionary service? Was this some sort of punishment for not being a better missionary? If he had not come on his mission, could he have kept this from happening?

Suddenly Elder Baker felt hypocritical. He was promising people that the gospel would bless their families, but his own family was falling apart. He was teaching people that families could be forever, but his own seemed to be ending. At times of discouragement in the past he had always turned to his parents. He wondered, *Where am I supposed to go now?* The minute he asked the question, he knew the answer: "Come unto me, all ye that labour and are heavy laden, and I will give you rest" (Matthew 11:28).

That week Elder Baker wrote me the following email:

"I'd be lying if I said that this week was anything but one of the toughest weeks ever. Life threw a pretty gnarly curveball that I sure didn't see coming. It's times like right now that I'm extra grateful for Jesus Christ—extra grateful for His Atonement. Without Him, man, I don't know how making it through life would be possible. He is so real. I know it. I felt it this week. I felt it more than I ever have before. His Atonement is so real. I've seen it firsthand. . . . Because of the Atonement of Jesus Christ, we can have the assurance that someone knows how we feel—always. I believe that on a dark night in a garden almost 2,000 years ago Christ felt every single pain, affliction, temptation, sickness, and infirmity that we would ever face or feel. He did it so we could have someone to turn to on hard days who actually knows how we feel. He did it so we could know that things will be okay. He did it out of complete love. Even when other loves fail and other foundations crumble, His love endures. His foundation is sure."

When you hear songs about a "holly, jolly Christmas" complete with "chestnuts roasting on an open fire" and "yuletide carols being sung by a choir," and the lyrics of the songs don't match your current circumstance, please don't lose heart. When choirs sing about sleigh rides and "a happy feeling nothing in the world can buy," don't feel disheartened. Don't think #Falseadvertising. Instead, think #Choosejoy. #ChooseChrist. For me, Christmas will always and forever be about the Christ in a cradle, the Messiah in a manger.

> For me, Christmas will always and forever be about the Christ in a cradle, the Messiah in a manger.

We hear the word *Messiah* often, and most of us understand it is another name for Jesus, but we don't always think about what the word means. *Messiah* is a Hebrew title that is equivalent to the English word *Christ*. It means "anointed one." That is why we sing, "O Jesus, the anointed, to thee our love we bring" (*Hymns*, no. 197).

An anointing sets in motion a future reality. Latter-day Saints are unique among Christians because we understand a premortal existence where Jesus was literally anointed by God the Father to be our Savior and Redeemer (see D&C 138:42; Bible Dictionary, "Anointed One"). He was anointed to do what only a God could do—to live a perfect life and fulfill the Atonement. He was also anointed to do what only a human could do—to live, learn, experience mortality, and die. The fulfillment of both aspects of His anointing started with His birth.

In this book, I invite you to make Christmas "merry and bright" by deepening your appreciation of the "Saviour, which is Christ the Lord" (Luke 2:11). Let us reflect on Christ and His gifts but also on the perspectives of some who were close to Him at His birth, in Book of Mormon times, and in Joseph Smith's day, as well as those who are His disciples today. Because of the Messiah in a manger, we can welcome light, grace, immortality, and eternal life. We can know God. Because of the Messiah in a manger, we have a Good Shepherd who cares for us and allows us to help Him care for others. Our love for Him deepens because of temples, the Book of Mormon, and Joseph Smith, who restored the gospel in our day. Because of the Messiah in a manger, we can follow modern prophets and, like them, live lives full of service and love. Christmas matters. Happiness and joy matter. Our choices matter. Our motives matter. We matter—all because of the Messiah in a manger.

CHRIST AND
HIS GIFTS

LIGHT OF THE WORLD

I love Christmas lights. Whether they are outdoors on homes or indoors on banisters and fireplace mantels, I love the magical glow that radiates from these lights during the Christmas season. Whether I see millions of lights on Temple Square or a single string on the wall of a missionary's apartment, Christmas lights make me happy.

The tradition of Christmas lights dates back to the seventeenth century, when Christians started putting candles on Christmas trees in Germany. The first electric lights on a Christmas tree came in 1882, when the vice president of Edison Electric Light Company had eighty red, white, and blue walnut-sized light bulbs specially made and wired together to adorn his family tree. In 1895, U.S. President Grover Cleveland put electric lights on the White House Christmas tree, and by the beginning of the twentieth century, the practice was commonplace. By the 1950s, electric lights were displayed not just on trees but along streets and on buildings and homes. Today we see lights in all shapes and sizes. Some are made to resemble icicles, snowflakes, or even meteor showers. People display lights in the shapes of snowmen, nutcrackers, and penguins. They twinkle, pulsate to music, and even blink out Christmas greetings in Morse code! In all the festive fun, let us not forget the lights are meant to remind us of Christ, who is the Light of the World.

> *In all the festive fun, let us not forget the lights are meant to remind us of Christ, who is the Light of the World.*

Some teach that Jesus gave Himself that title when He declared, "I am the light of the world: he that followeth me shall not walk in darkness, but shall have the light of life" (John 8:12). However, Latter-day Saints know Christ was not *giving* Himself a title, but *reminding* followers of a title that was already His. It was He who said, "Let there be light" in the beginning and then "divided the light from the darkness" (Moses 2:3–4). It is Christ who gives "light to every man that cometh into the world" (D&C 84:46). People can label that light a conscience or an inborn moral compass, but we know it is the "light of Christ" (Alma 28:14; Moroni 7:18; D&C 88:7). Some may not recognize His light or may deny it completely, but Jesus

Christ's influence in every life has been and will always be deliberate and dynamic.

Traditionally, artists have depicted Christ with a halo or with light shining on or from His face. These portrayals are in tune with the words of modern prophets. Joseph Smith described God the Father and Jesus Christ, whose "brightness and glory defy all description" (JS–H 1:17). The Prophet wrote of Christ: "His eyes were as a flame of fire; the hair of his head was white like the pure snow; his countenance shone above the brightness of the sun" (D&C 110:3). President Lorenzo Snow shared a similar witness. His granddaughter, Allie Young Pond, recorded that her grandfather showed her the exact spot in the Salt Lake Temple where the Savior had appeared to him and "described His hands, feet, countenance and beautiful, white robes, all of which were of such a glory of whiteness and brightness that he could hardly gaze upon Him."[1]

Christ emanates light. Artists have depicted it. Prophets have testified of it. Even the date we celebrate Christmas teaches of it. Though it may not be the exact date of Christ's birth, I am pleased that we join with Christians everywhere and

Christ emanates light. Artists have depicted it. Prophets have testified of it. Even the date we celebrate Christmas teaches of it.

5

celebrate that miracle in December, when those living in the northern hemisphere welcome an increase of light back into the world.

During summer, the North Pole of the earth is tilted toward the sun and daylight hours are prolonged. During winter, the North Pole is tilted away and daylight hours are shortened. The actual day when daylight is the shortest usually happens between December 20th and 23rd. That means that by the 24th and 25th when we celebrate Christmas, in the northern hemisphere, light has begun to fill the world once again.

Cultures from before the time of Christ traditionally celebrated the coming of light in both the northern and southern hemispheres. For example, the ancient Incas were vigilant in tracking the changing position of the earth in relation to the sun. I had always been told that this was because they were sun worshipers. When I had the opportunity to visit Machu Picchu in Peru, our guide explained that, more likely, they were agrarians who needed to know when it was time to plant and harvest their crops. Our guide showed us the remains of what he called the temple of the sun, in which there were two small windows. These openings were positioned such that on the winter and summer solstices, the sun's rays would pass directly through them and light the center of a sacrificial rock carved in the shape of an animal. They celebrated the coming of the sun. We celebrate the coming of the Son. They erected a sacrificial stone. We know Jesus was the ultimate sacrifice.

When Christ came to the Americas, He told the people they were no longer to sacrifice animals. Instead, He said, "Ye shall offer for a sacrifice unto me a broken heart and a contrite spirit. And whoso cometh unto me with a broken heart and a contrite spirit, him will I baptize with fire and with the Holy Ghost" (3 Nephi 9:20). This is the exchange that happens each week as we partake of the sacrament.

Some wonder, since Christmas lights are symbols of Jesus, why Latter-day Saints do not fill our chapels with them during Christmastime as other denominations sometimes do. I think the answer is that we already have the most important symbol of light in our chapels all year: the sacrament. Brent L. Top has written the following: "The Atonement of Jesus Christ, as symbolized by the sacramental bread and water, gives us light and life— in fact, the scriptures use the term 'light of life' (John 8:12). In an eternal sense, all will be given everlasting life through resurrection to a kingdom of glory. And as resurrected beings, all will possess light and glory in a very literal sense. The Savior's promises, however, are not just reserved in waiting for some far-off day in a far-off realm.

They are available right here and right now. As we covenant with the Lord through baptism, confirmation, the sacrament, and other ordinances, we commit to live our lives in harmony with His gospel. He covenants with us to fill our lives with spiritual light and abundant life."[2]

As we understand the sacrament in this way, we can have Christ's Spirit to be with us and be filled with light (see D&C 20:77, 79). People often speak about the moment when "the light goes on," but the truth is that the light goes in.

> *People often speak about the moment when "the light goes on," but the truth is that the light goes in.*

I have witnessed that wonderful moment on many occasions. Once was when I first met Jeremy Guthrie. Jeremy is an LDS professional baseball pitcher who played for five different major league teams before retiring in 2017. In 2012 he started pitching for the Kansas City Royals and helped the team become World Series champions in 2015. Jeremy was born and grew up in Oregon, but I first met him at a session of Especially for Youth held at BYU when he was a teenager. I did not know this young man was a high school all-star in basketball, football, baseball, and academics. I just noticed how intently he was listening during my classes. I knew he had felt the Spirit. I saw the light go in.

After one of the classes, I pulled him aside and told him he would be a great missionary. I challenged him to not let anything get in the way of that. Jeremy now says those were the words that ran through his mind when he was offered a million-dollar contract to play baseball if he would forego his mission. Jeremy rejected the contract, put in his mission papers, and was called to Spain, where he served faithfully for two years.

Contrary to what some may have predicted, Jeremy's mission did not hold him back from pursuing a professional baseball career. He claims his mission gave him the added maturity, focus, and willingness to work hard that helped him succeed. These same attributes led to a strong marriage and family. He and his amazing wife, Jenny, have three great kids who will soon be old enough to begin attending EFY themselves. The family recently moved to Texas, where Jeremy is presiding over the Houston South Mission.

Jeremy Guthrie is known for being a brilliant and talented baseball pitcher, and I admire his athletic accomplishments as much as anyone. He is a wonderful mission president. However, to me, Jeremy will always be a valiant young teenager who recognized and followed the Spirit—a young man who welcomed the light.

Some children are afraid of the dark, but, sadly, some

adults are afraid of the light. Maybe it reminds them of what they have lost. Perhaps they are afraid of the responsibilities that come with Christ's light. Sometimes they simply have become so comfortable in the dark that facing the light is painful. Of such, the Lord has said, "They love darkness rather than light, . . . therefore they will not ask of me" (D&C 10:21).

> *Some children are afraid of the dark, but, sadly, some adults are afraid of the light.*

May every Christmas light we see remind us to ask the Lord for His help, strength, and direction. Let every light on every house, building, and branch remind us to welcome light into the world by celebrating the Light of the World.

Because of the Messiah in a manger, each time we partake of the sacrament we can bring our broken hearts and contrite spirits to Him and be filled with His light. In Doctrine and Covenants we read, "That which is of God is light; and he that receiveth light, and continueth in God, receiveth more light." Because of the Messiah in a manger, we can feel the light go in and then invite more and more "until the perfect day" (D&C 50:24).

THE LEGEND OF
THE POINSETTIA

A re we allowed to choose a favorite Christmas
symbol? It's almost as tricky as picking a favorite
General Authority, scripture, or hymn. Nevertheless, I
choose poinsettias. I love the vivid green and red colors
that surround us each December. I even love poinsettias
when they are white, pink, or marbled. Most of all, I love
the legend of how we got poinsettias in the first place.

The flower came from Mexico, where it is called *flor
de Nochebuena*—the Flower of the Holy Night. It was first
brought to the United States by Joel Roberts Poinsett in
1830. That's how it got its English name, and since 1830
is the same year the Church was organized, I think it
should have a little extra meaning for Latter-day Saints.

According to the legend, the first *flor de Nochebuena*
appeared many years ago in a small Mexican village
where people were preparing to celebrate Christmas.

As the special day approached, the local priest asked a woman in his parish to weave a blanket to place beneath the statue of the baby Jesus at the church on Christmas Eve. The woman's daughter, Luz, felt proud that her mother had been chosen for such an honor, but as Christmas drew nearer, Luz's mother became gravely ill. Her father prepared to take his wife to the hospital far away in the big city. Luz was worried about her mother, but also about the blanket.

Discerning her thoughts, Luz's father said, "The priest will have to understand." But Luz worried that the priest would not understand, and neither would their friends and neighbors. Everyone was counting on her mother, and now they would have nothing for the baby Jesus on Christmas Eve. Luz determined to finish the weaving on her own. But the harder she tried, the worse the blanket became, until eventually it was nothing more than a tangled mess.

When Christmas Eve came, instead of going to the church, Luz hid behind her small house. An old woman saw her and approached. "What's wrong, child?" the woman asked.

"I have nothing to take for the procession of the gifts," Luz sobbed. "My mother was supposed to weave the blanket for the manger, but she became sick, and now there is nothing to place beneath the baby Jesus."

The old woman pointed to the weeds growing nearby and said, "Take those. They will make a comfortable bed for the baby."

Luz stared at the woman in disbelief. How could she take weeds to the Savior?

The old woman explained, "Any gift is beautiful when it is given with love." She gathered an armful of weeds and held

Any gift is beautiful when it is given with love.

them out to Luz, who obediently took them and headed to the church.

When Luz entered the church, she heard the people gasp as they saw her carrying weeds instead of the ex-pected blanket. Luz thought about turning to leave, but the priest smiled and beckoned for her to continue forward. She approached the manger and gently placed the weeds around the statue of baby Jesus. As she did, suddenly the green weeds were tipped with beautiful red leaves. They looked like flaming stars. The manger be-gan to glow and shimmer as if lit by hundreds of candles. A hush fell over the congregation. The old woman was right. Any gift is beautiful when it is given with love. And—according to the legend—every Christmas since that day, the red stars have shone atop green branches in Mexico and all over the world.[3]

I love this story and have shared it many times through the years. The legend is a beautiful reminder of the love with which we should give gifts to each other, but also of the gift of grace the Savior lovingly gives to us. In the legend, the weeds were made beautiful, and that is exactly how Christ can change and transform us. "Be not conformed to this world," Paul wrote, "but be ye transformed" (Romans 12:2). Because of grace—divine help—not only can we repent, be resurrected, and return to God, but we can become "partakers of the divine nature" (2 Peter 1:4).

Sometimes we become so comfortable with how we are now we don't recognize the need for change. We become content with being weeds and forget that God has something better in store for us. Elder Neal A. Maxwell taught, "The Lord loves each of us too much to merely let us go on being what we now are, for He knows what we have the possibility to become."[4]

Then something happens to remind us we can be better than we are. One of those reminders came to me when I was given a gift certificate to take my family out for a nice dinner.

I now offer a public apology to every server who has

ever taken care of my family in a restaurant. My dad and mom reared four sons on teachers' salaries. We didn't eat out much, and when we did, it always ended in a tug-of-war between my parents as to the size of the tip. Mom was generous; Dad was frugal. What neither of them knew was that my younger brother and I would usually pocket whatever amount they finally left on the table once they walked away. We just couldn't see why Mom and Dad would leave perfectly good money on the table for a stranger when we could use it to buy candy! We were horrible. Dear former servers: If you ever cleaned up a table and found no tip, don't blame my parents. It was my brother and me!

I did better as I got older, but I'm still far from where I need to be. The Mom part of me always wants to leave a nice tip, but the Dad part knows my resources are limited. Thank heaven God gave me my wife, Debi, who keeps me in line.

On the night I took my family out to use the gift certificate, we enjoyed a great meal and then asked the server to bring the bill. He informed us that it had already been covered. Someone in the restaurant had told the server he was a former student of mine and generously paid for our meal. I couldn't believe it. I quickly started looking around the restaurant trying to identify the person we needed to thank. Just then, I heard Debi say to our server, "Then let us just leave this gift certificate as your tip." It would have been a perfect moment worthy of mention in the *Ensign* magazine—mystery student pays for teacher's meal, so teacher, in turn, leaves large tip for server. Yes, it would have been an ideal story—except I had to ruin it by blurting out (right in front of the server), "You're giving him the *whole* gift certificate?"

You don't have to strangle me. My kids already did it for you. In my defense, I believed the gift certificate was for a lot more than it actually was. But even so, why couldn't my knee-jerk reaction have been to return grace for grace? Why couldn't I have been as generous to our server as the person who had given us the gift certificate in the first place or the former student who had paid our bill? For the record, we did leave the server the gift certificate, but the experience reminded me of how far I have to go when it comes to being Christlike. It reminded me that I am a weed and desperately need Christ to turn me into a poinsettia.

Although I'm no longer the kid who pocketed the tips his parents left, I need to become the guy who says, "Take the whole gift certificate." Whether or not I can afford to give extravagant gifts is not the point. I want whatever gift I offer to be given without one self-ish thought—to flow naturally out of a full and grateful heart. I can't make such a change happen on my own. I am totally dependent on my Savior to squeeze selfishness out of me and replace it with His charity.

Because of the Messiah in a manger, we can be changed. Without Christ's grace, we would be forever aware of our shortcomings with no way to improve them—forever cast as villains despite our heartfelt desires to be heroes, forever weeds rather than poinsettias. Because of the Messiah in a manger, our hearts, minds, and very natures can be changed. We can be made holy.

Elder D. Todd Christofferson has taught that the Savior's atoning grace can take away our sins, but beyond that, it also allows us to "internalize the qualities and character of Christ." He said, "We cannot be content to remain as we are but must be moving constantly toward 'the measure of the stature of the fulness of Christ' (Ephesians 4:13)."[5]

In scripture the Lord commanded, "Be ye holy; for I am holy" (1 Peter 1:16). Elder Christofferson also explained that early Saints wrote the words

> *"Holiness to the Lord" can become holiness like the Lord. As we give ourselves to God in love, He can turn weeds into poinsettias.*

"Holiness to the Lord" not only on temples but also on items as common as hammers, drums, and doorknobs.[6] I have never seen a poinsettia that bears the inscription "Holiness to the Lord," but the Flower of the Holy Night reminds me that because of the Messiah in a manger, "Holiness to the Lord" can become holiness *like* the Lord. As we give ourselves to God in love, He can turn weeds into poinsettias.

THE TREES OF
CHRISTMAS

A cherished memory from childhood is when Grandma Camenish would gather up whichever grandkids were around and let us help pick out her Christmas tree. My parents always had an artificial tree, but Grandma loved getting a real one. We would head to the tree lot the Baum family set up in their front yard and search through row after row until we finally settled on just the right one. Brother Baum would help us rope the tree to the top of Grandma's car, and off we went.

At Grandma's house, we divided and conquered. Some of the cousins untied the tree and worked on getting it into the stand while the rest of us ran upstairs and hauled decorations—some of them antiques even back then—out of cupboards. We draped the tree with lights, strings of beads, and ornaments while Grandma supervised. The final product was always a hodgepodge mixture of handmade and store-bought decorations, but she would say it was "just perfect" and then give her annual reminder: The tradition of Christmas trees began in Germany, where Christians used the evergreen fir trees as a symbol of Christ's gift of everlasting life.

Today, Grandma's reminder seems more needed than ever. For too many, Christmas trees have become just another holiday trimming with little or no connection to Christ. We see Christmas trees in movies, shopping malls, and airports, but they lack meaning until people see "beyond the symbol, the mighty realities for which the symbols stand."[7] Christmas trees become most meaningful when we consider them in the context of what I call the other trees of Christmas: trees found in the Gardens of Eden and Gethsemane, the tree that was the cross, and the trees that filled the Sacred Grove.

In the Garden of Eden there were two significant trees: the tree of knowledge of good and evil and the tree of life. Adam and Eve were given freedom to choose between them. They could stay where they were or go. They could stay as they were or grow. The tree of life offered immortality, but without the possibility of progression. By choosing to partake of the fruit of the tree of knowledge of good and evil, our first parents selected the more difficult road, but the only one worth traveling.

After Adam and Eve partook of the fruit, God sent angels to guard the tree of life—not to punish Adam and Eve, but because if they had partaken of its fruit at that point, they would have lived forever in their sins. Angels and a flaming sword pointed our first parents away from the tree of life and toward the Atonement of Jesus Christ, through which they— and all of us—can not only live forever but can repent and live

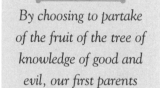

By choosing to partake of the fruit of the tree of knowledge of good and evil, our first parents selected the more difficult road, but the only one worth traveling.

with and *like* God. Christmas trees have more meaning for me when I remember the trees in the Garden of Eden.

In the Garden of Gethsemane, olive trees surrounded the Savior as He prayed. There Jesus mercifully took upon Himself every violation of justice and every pain, affliction, temptation, and sickness ever experienced (see Alma 7:11). Christ suffered for the sins of those who loved Him, those who hated Him, and even those who would never know Him in this life. Like the fir trees we use as Christmas trees, olive trees are also evergreen. They don't lose their leaves, and when they are cut down, new branches grow from the roots. As we make and renew covenants with Christ, our discipleship is evergreen. Christmas trees have more meaning for me when I remember the olive trees in Gethsemane.

> *Christ suffered for the sins of those who loved Him, those who hated Him, and even those who would never know Him in this life.*

Christ's cross is often called a tree. Peter and John testified to the Jews, "The God of our fathers raised up Jesus, whom ye slew and hanged on a tree" (Acts 5:30). In Gethsemane, an angel was sent to sustain Christ, but on the cross He was alone. Even the Father withdrew, so that the payment would be complete. The cross became the only tree to witness a forsaken Savior. Zenos's allegory about olive trees in the Book of Mormon was a long answer to a short question: "How is it possible that [the Jews], after having rejected the sure foundation, can ever build upon it, that it may become the head of their corner?" (Jacob 4:17). In other words, what hope is there for those who reject Christ? In the allegory, we are assured that the Lord will mercifully provide many opportunities for everyone to get it right before the end comes. Christ died for all people, and then He visited the spirit world to begin preaching the gospel to all who had died without it. Christmas trees have more meaning for me when I remember the tree that was the cross.

Let us not forget the trees that filled the Sacred Grove. On a soft spring morning in 1820, a young Joseph Smith sought privacy among those trees to pray. Satan thought if he could bind this young man's tongue and keep his questions forever unasked, then he could overturn the righteous choice of Eden and render ineffectual the blood spilt in Gethsemane and on Calvary. But just when Joseph was about to surrender himself to destruction, he saw a pillar of light. The trees around him shimmered as if they were on fire. God and Christ appeared and ushered in the Restoration. Priesthood keys and essential ordinances soon followed. The blessings of the Atonement were at long last within reach for us, our ancestors, and all God's children. Christmas trees have more meaning for me when I remember the trees in the Sacred Grove.

I'm thankful for Christmas trees, but also for what I see as the additional trees of Christmas. Because of Adam and Eve's choice in the Garden of Eden, the door was opened for progression. Because of Christ's suffering in Gethsemane and on Calvary, the door was opened for us to have immortality and the possibility of eternal life. Because of the Restoration, the door was opened for the fulness of the gospel in preparation for the Second Coming.

I loved my grandmother's Christmas trees through the years. I enjoyed gathering with my cousins to pick them out, set them up, and decorate them. Most of all, I am glad Grandma never let the significance of the Christmas tree stop there. She always bore testimony that the reason for those evergreen trees was to remind us of the everlasting life we have because of the Messiah in a manger.

HOLY FAMILY

SON OF THE BLESSED

One of the many titles of Jesus Christ is "Son of the Blessed" (Mark 14:61), referring to His blessed mother, Mary. Mary has been portrayed in many ways through art and literature across the centuries, but one of my favorite portrayals of her is in a beloved children's book called *Wombat Divine*, by Mem Fox, an Australian author. In the story, a group of Australian animals is putting on the Nativity play. The emu is in charge and casts koalas as shepherds, kangaroos as wise men, and a wombat as baby Jesus.[1] The part of Mary is played by a numbat. This rare Australian animal is also called a banded anteater. It's small, has stripes on its furry back, and eats termites—an odd choice for Mary, until you realize this animal is known for two characteristics: its beauty and the great lengths it goes to in order to protect its young. Good choice for Mary after all.

In the Book of Mormon, Mary is described as "exceedingly fair" (1 Nephi 11:13), but she was also exceedingly brave and resilient. Not every young woman could have stood up to the gossip and derision that surely accompanied the unique circumstances surrounding Christ's birth. Mary had to be a strong girl to make the trip from Nazareth to Bethlehem when she was nine months pregnant. Her strength was needed again when she and Joseph escaped to Egypt in order to keep Jesus safe from Herod. Living in a different country and raising her son far from home and family could not have been easy for her. Mary was an extraordinary woman.

When Nephi sought to know the meaning of Lehi's dream, the Spirit showed him Mary: "Behold, the virgin whom thou seest is the mother of the son of God, after the manner of the flesh" (1 Nephi 11:18). Then the Spirit said, "Look! And [he] looked and beheld the virgin again, bearing a child in her arms. . . . Yea, even the Son of the Eternal Father!" (1 Nephi 11:19–21). Think of it! When the Spirit was trying to teach Nephi about the love of God, He showed him a woman! Similarly, Elder Jeffrey R. Holland declared, "No love in mortality comes closer to approximating the pure love of Jesus Christ than the selfless love a devoted mother has for her child."[2]

My son-in-law Gian was once given the unenviable

task of speaking in sacrament meeting on Mother's Day. He worried that if he spoke about the goodness of his own mother and wife, other women might feel bad. He knew that if he spoke about his mother's and wife's shortcomings, they would feel bad. He decided to speak about mothers in general and how their love leads us to the Savior. I thought the insight he shared that day was profound. God knew there would be lots of people born on this earth with no awareness of Jesus Christ—that millions would have to wait until the spirit world to learn about the Savior. Since everyone could not be given a knowledge of the Savior, God gave every soul a mother. Maybe He hoped that through some of these mothers, He could give all His children a taste of the selfless sacrifice and perfect love of Christ. Perhaps it is through the love of good mothers that God prepares all of His children to one day recognize and accept the love of their good Savior.

Nephi was asked, "Knowest thou the condescension of God?" (1 Nephi 11:16). We typically think of the condescension of God only in terms of Christ's willingness to "descend from his throne divine" (*Hymns*, no. 193) and mildly lay "his

> *Perhaps it is through the love of good mothers that God prepares all of His children to one day recognize and accept the love of their good Savior.*

glory by" (*Hymns*, no. 209). We sometimes think of the Father's willingness to let Christ come to atone for us. However, Their condescension was still dependent on Mary's willingness to obey.

Mary was a young girl when an angel appeared and told her God had a special work for her to do (see Luke 1:31). In the Bible we learn the angel's name was Gabriel (see Luke 1:26). Joseph Smith taught that Gabriel is none other than Noah.[3] It was Noah who told Mary to not be afraid (see Luke 1:30). Perhaps he remembered how frightened he had been when heavenly messengers had come to him (see Genesis 6). Noah had received his own difficult task from the Lord. He knew that what lay ahead of Mary would not be easy. He knew people would misjudge and ridicule her. He had faced similar rejection. How happy it must have made Noah, the very prophet who saw the destruction of the world, to be able to announce the salvation of the world. Noah prepared the ark that saved his family. Mary prepared the "ark" that would save God's family.

> Noah prepared the ark that saved his family. Mary prepared the "ark" that would save God's family.

Yet, salvation could have been halted had Mary been unwilling. Heavenly Father would not pressure her. It had to be her choice. Thankfully, her immediate response to the angel was willingness. Elder Holland said, "The nature of [Mary's] spirit and the depth of her preparation were revealed in a response that shows both innocence and maturity: 'Behold the handmaid of the Lord; be it unto me according to thy word' (Luke 1:38)."[4] Mary chose to fulfill her divinely appointed role because she loved God, Christ, and us. God and Mary both loved us enough to send their only begotten Son, and Jesus loved us enough to become the "only begotten Son, that whosoever believeth in him should not perish, but have everlasting life" (John 3:16).

These were not fictional characters in a children's book about the Nativity. These were not animals taking on human roles. This was not a play or pageant. It was real. Because of the Messiah who condescended to be born in a manger, we were offered salvation. However, that could not have happened without the meekness and righteous choice of His mother. Christ is called the Son of the Blessed—the blessed mother Mary. In her love we gain a sense of "the love of God, which sheddeth itself abroad in the hearts of the children of men; wherefore, it is the most desirable above all things . . . and the most joyous to the soul" (1 Nephi 11:22–23).

SWADDLING CLOTHES, MANGERS, AND INNS

A nd [Mary] brought forth her firstborn son, and wrapped him in swaddling clothes, and laid him in a manger; because there was no room for them in the inn" (Luke 2:7). The words are so familiar that most of us can recite them from memory. Nevertheless, they take on greater significance when we look more deeply into the meaning of swaddling clothes, mangers, and inns.

Swaddling clothes are narrow bands of cloth wrapped around a newborn. This was commonly done to restrain the baby's movements so he would not scratch or harm himself. However, in Jesus' case, there was an additional purpose. Angels said the swaddling clothes would be a sign of Christ's true identity (see Luke 2:12). How could that be, since most babies at the time were swaddled?

John W. Welch has taught of the possibility that swaddling bands were marked to identify whose baby it was.[5] Parents must have worried back then about the possibility of babies being switched just as they do today. Marking swaddling bands reduced those chances. Sometimes in Jewish weddings, the hands of the couple are tied loosely together with cloth bands that have been embroidered with symbols or tokens representing their family histories. That's how we got the saying, "Tying the knot." Could these very bands used at the wedding also be used by the couple to fasten the swaddling clothes of their newborn children?

We know Joseph and Mary were of the "house and lineage of David" (Luke 2:4). Zechariah had proclaimed that the Lord "raised up an horn of salvation for us in the house of his servant David" (Luke 1:69). Could it be that the swaddling clothes around Jesus were bands made of the royal colors of blue and white, in declaration of Christ's Davidic lineage? Could it be that the swaddling clothes around Jesus were held with bands embroidered with lions or lambs, common images of the tribe of Judah? Such swaddling clothes would surely have been unique and could have more easily identified Jesus to the shepherds.

Whether or not Jesus' swaddling bands were colored or embroidered with family symbols, they were definitely a sign of His entrance into full humanity. John W. Welch also wrote, "That the Lord Jehovah would become flesh as a helpless child and was swaddled like any other infant is an exquisite manifestation of his unfathomable conde-scension."[6]

Along with learning more about swaddling clothes, let us also learn about mangers. Mangers are troughs from which animals eat. The English noun *manger* comes from the French verb *manger*, which means "to eat." Despite the number of European-style wooden mangers we have seen portrayed in pictures and Christmas cards, Christ's manger was probably made of stone. Wood was too scarce in the desert climate of the Holy Land to be used for ani-mals. Angels said the Lord would be "lying in a manger" (Luke 2:16). Many mothers swaddled their babies, but they didn't lay them in mangers. This would have been a sure sign to the shepherds that they had found Jesus.

As Mary and Joseph laid Christ in a trough from which animals ate, they were foreshadowing what Christ Himself would later teach: "He that eateth my flesh, and drinketh my blood, dwelleth in me, and I in him" (John 6:56). Bethlehem means "House of Bread." It was also Jerusalem's water source. What a fitting place for the birth of the "bread of life" (John 6:35) and "living water" (John 4:10).

Just as animals go to the manger for physical food, we go to the Savior for spiritual nourishment. We need never go hungry. We need never thirst. We need only "come and partake" (Alma 42:27). That is the invitation of Christ. That is the invitation of Christmas.

> We need never go hungry. We need never thirst. We need only "come and partake" (Alma 42:27). That is the invitation of Christ. That is the invitation of Christmas.

In addition to learning about swaddling clothes and mangers, we need to understand inns. The inns in Jesus' time were different from the motels and hotels of today. According to the American Bible Society, there were at least three types of inns in Christ's time. Some inns were large rooms in which travelers were given a safe place to stretch out on the ground around a fire. Sleeping with a roomful of strangers was far from ideal, but it was better than being unprotected from robbers and the elements. Another type of inn was a public building where travelers paid money for food and lodging. This was the type of inn Jesus referred to in the parable of the good Samaritan (see Luke 10:34). Sometimes inns referred to guest rooms people had in their homes. The Greek word *kataluma*, translated as "upper room" in the description of the Last Supper (Mark 14:15), was the exact same word translated as "inn" in Luke 2. In both cases, it could have been translated as "guest room."

Since Bethlehem was not along a regular trade route, the inn we read about in Luke 2 was probably not a large room full of strangers or a public building for wealthy travelers. Instead, it was probably a guest room in the home of one of Joseph's relatives. The census was going on. The small town was crowded with visitors who were all related. No wonder guest rooms were full to over-flowing. Perhaps "no room for them in the inn" (Luke 2:7) was not so much a statement about people's lack of hospitality as it was a statement of fact. However, BYU professor of ancient scripture Tyler Griffin has suggested another explanation. Maybe these relatives had done the math and realized that the time of Mary's delivery was not jiving with the time of her marriage. Maybe their rejection was in judgment and condemnation. After all, wouldn't relatives make room for a family member in labor even if it meant that other relatives whose needs were less pressing had to vacate the guest room?[7] In the Joseph Smith Translation of the Bible, the Prophet changed *inn* to *inns*. Making the word plural indicated that this couple was being rejected by everyone. Maybe the words in Luke 2:7 that tell the true story are *for them*—there was "no room *for them* in the inns" (emphasis added). Whatever the case, Mary and Joseph prepared to deliver a baby in a stable—probably a cave—used for animals.

Swaddling clothes, mangers, and inns—all very interesting, but what do they mean for us today? We may not swaddle infants in exactly the same way, place them in stone mangers, or have guest rooms or stables. However, we still need to recognize Christ and find room for Him. We will not know Him from tokens embroidered on swaddling bands but by the tokens in His hands and feet (see 1 Nephi 21:16). We will not find Him in a stone manger but at the head of His Church (see D&C 1:38). We not only need to make room for Him in our homes but in our hearts.

The observation made by Elder Neal A. Maxwell in 1995 is even truer today: "For many moderns, sad to say, the query 'What think ye of Christ?' (Matthew 22:42) would be answered, 'I really don't think of Him at all!'"[8] Yet the Lord has said, "Behold, I stand at the door, and knock; if any man hear my voice, and open the door, I will come in to him, and will sup with him, and he with me" (Revelation 3:20).

Because the Messiah is no longer in a manger, on a cross, or in a tomb, He can help us overcome the world. He has said, "To him that overcometh will I grant to sit with me in my throne, even as I also overcame, and am set down with my Father in his throne" (Revelation 3:21).

NOEL, KNOW WELL

"The first Noel the angel did say was to certain poor shepherds in fields as they lay" (*Hymns*, no. 213). Most people know that the word *Noël* is French for "Christmas," but the word can be traced back even further to the Latin *natalis*, meaning "birthday." The text of the hymn reminds us that the first Christmas was Jesus' birthday. Mary and Joseph were there with a few shepherds and "a multitude of the heavenly host praising God, and saying, Glory to God in the highest, and on earth peace, good will toward men" (Luke 2:13–14).

Many years have passed since the first Noel, and mankind is still struggling to find the peace and good will the angels proclaimed. Surely it is in part because many fail to grasp the promise of salvation and the divine potential made possible by the Savior, but perhaps it is also because most people do not yet know the God the angels praised and sang about, the true Father of the baby in the manger. Mary is His mother, but Joseph was only a trustworthy and loving guardian. God was the Father of Christ's body as well as His spirit.

Although the vast majority of people on Earth profess some sort of belief in God or a higher power, they don't know God well enough to access His power. For many, their belief in God rarely affects their daily choices or makes a positive difference in their lives. That's one of the reasons I love Christmas so much. Christmas serves as an annual wake-up call. Each Noel is truly an invitation for us to know God well.[9]

> *Christmas serves as an annual wake-up call. Each Noel is truly an invitation for us to know God well.*

Mucioko Banza was born and reared in the Democratic Republic of the Congo. He came from a religious family and received a scholarship from his church to study in Switzerland. He and his wife and two children moved to Geneva, where he pursued his university studies and participated fully in his church. Still, Mucioko had questions no one in his church had ever been able to answer to his satisfaction: "What is the nature of God? Who is He really? What does He look like?" Mucioko said, "I had been told He was everything, in everything, incomprehensible—basically a being we could not relate to or even understand."[10] Mucioko needed something more. He reasoned that if God exists and if He is loving, surely He will reach out to us and let us know who He is and what He desires of us.

Mucioko met a friend who told him he had heard missionaries teach of a man who had seen God. Mucioko's curiosity was piqued. When he met the missionaries, they taught him about Joseph Smith's First Vision. Mucioko said, "Here was the answer to my questions about the nature of God. He is our Father and He has a body of flesh and bones. We look like Him. . . . [Joseph Smith] saw Him and talked to Him!"[11]

Mucioko and his wife learned that God, Jesus, and the Holy Ghost are united in purpose but separate and distinct individuals and that They have a plan for our lives. We have purpose beyond just existing and dying. We lived before we were born, we are on earth for a reason, and we will continue to live and progress after we die. Mucioko began feeling great joy as he learned more about God's plan and chose to live in accordance with it.

Many religious leaders believe in God and encourage others to do the same. However, it is one thing to believe in God and another thing to *know* Him. Jesus prayed to His Father and said, "And this is life eternal, that they might know thee the only true God, and Jesus Christ, whom thou hast sent" (John 17:3). Missionaries taught Mucioko and his family to know God, and that made all the difference. They joined The Church of Jesus Christ of Latter-day Saints in Switzerland, returned to their country in

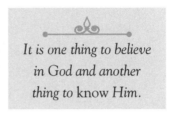

It is one thing to believe in God and another thing to know Him.

Africa, and were influential in obtaining formal recognition for the LDS Church there. Now there are over 50,000 members in the Democratic Republic of the Congo.

On April 7, 1844, Joseph Smith declared, "There are but a very few beings in the world who understand rightly the character of God. The great majority of mankind do not comprehend anything, either that which is past, or that which is to come, [in regards to] their relationship to God. . . . If men do not comprehend the character of God, they do not comprehend themselves."[12]

In 2017, I served as the moderator of an interfaith dialogue held at Brigham Young University between an evangelical leader and a BYU religion professor, Anthony Sweat. Both speakers shared similar views when asked about Jesus' life, teachings, death, and Resurrection. However, stark differences surfaced when they were asked to describe the nature of God. The evangelical leader said God is "invisible" and "unknowable." He described God as a totally different species than man—as different from us as animals are from humans and as distant from us as the farthest star. I realize he did not speak for all evangelicals, but I couldn't help but feel saddened by his words. I was grateful when Brother Sweat said, "Latter-day Saints believe that God is visible and knowable. He is as close to us as we will allow Him to be. Not only are we the same species, but He is the literal Father of our spirits and we are His beloved children."

> *This student had sung "I am a child of God" his entire life, but he had not realized how unique and meaningful the doctrine communicated in those words truly is.*

After the event was over, one of my students sought me out and said, "Brother Wilcox, I finally realize why the Restoration was needed. People had lost the true knowledge of God. Heavenly Father Himself had to come and straighten them out." This student had sung "I am a child of God" his entire life, but he had not realized how unique and meaningful the doctrine communicated in those words truly is.

Because of the Messiah in a manger, we can know God. Jesus provides a true knowledge of the nature of God and our relationship to Him. Elder Jeffrey R. Holland testified, "Of the many magnificent purposes served in the life and ministry of the Lord Jesus Christ, one . . . is the grand truth that in all that Jesus came to say and do, including and especially in His atoning suffering and sacrifice, He was showing us who and what God our Eternal Father is like. . . . In word and in deed Jesus was trying to reveal and make personal to us the true nature of His Father, our Father in Heaven."[13]

This knowledge brings purpose and security. God is not some ethereal and nebulous force in the universe. He did not just create the earth and then refuse to tell us why. He is not some sort of mad scientist who is experimenting with us or a tyrant who enjoys watching us suffer. He did not create us for His amusement, to keep Him company, or simply to have something beneath Himself to worship Him. As the Young Women theme reminds us, "We are [children] of our Heavenly Father, who loves us, and we love Him."[14] We know God because we know Christ, who was and is in "the express image of his [Father]" (Hebrews 1:3). Because of the Messiah in a manger, not only can we sing "The First Noel," but we can know God well.

SHEPHERDS
AND ANGELS

THE GOOD SHEPHERD

Each December we read about "shepherds abiding in the field, keeping watch over their flock by night" (Luke 2:8). Children imitate the shepherds by wearing bathrobes and holding cardboard crooks, but most people know little about what shepherds actually did in Christ's time and why the Savior referred to Himself as the "good shepherd" (John 10:11).

Not too long ago, I had the opportunity to direct a tour to the Holy Land, and we stopped at the shepherds' fields just outside of Bethlehem. I love the location because it still looks the same as it must have appeared 2,000 years ago. As we overlooked the fields we couldn't help but sing Christmas carols, even though it was the middle of June.

After the songs, our local guide talked to us about shepherds. Each tour group in Israel is required to have a local guide. Sometimes I have traveled with Palestinian Muslims, but this guide was a Palestinian Christian named Sam. His insights touched my heart.

Sam talked about how shepherding in ancient Israel was difficult and demanding work—a twenty-four-hour-a-day job. There were always people who were willing to do the work for money, but they lacked the dedication and devotion shown by shepherds who actually owned their sheep. No wonder we read in scripture, "The hireling fleeth, because he is an hireling, and careth not for the sheep" (John 10:13).

Sam drew our attention to the caves that pockmarked the hills across from us. "These were sheepfolds at night," he explained. In Christ's time, shepherds typically had small flocks of thirty to fifty sheep so they could separate from each other during the day and not overrun the same pastures and water sources. But at night they brought the flocks together to protect them from wolves, jackals, and robbers. Some of the caves held over two hundred sheep. Several shepherds would work together to block the front of a cave with stones, leaving only a narrow entrance through which one or two sheep could pass at a time. The shepherds would then lead the sheep into the fold and rotate guard duty by taking turns sitting so as to block the entrance to the cave while the others slept. Sam said, "The shepherd on duty didn't just guard the door. He became the door." No wonder the Savior said, "I am the door of the sheep" (John 10:7) and "he that entereth not by the door into the sheepfold . . . the same is a thief and a robber" (John 10:1).

By morning, sheep from different flocks had mixed together. No one knew which sheep belonged to which shepherd until the shepherds took turns standing at the entrance and whistling or calling in their own distinct ways. Then each shepherd's sheep would recognize the call and come forward. As sheep passed through the narrow entrance, the shepherd would count them and make sure none was missed. Remember that the Savior said, "My sheep hear my voice, and I know them, and they follow me" (John 10:27).

Anciently, the shepherd carried a rod and a staff. The rod was a club like a baseball bat, and the shepherd would use it to beat away predators if they approached the flock. Just seeing the rod in the shepherd's hand made the sheep feel safe and secure. The staff was a long pole that he used to support himself while walking across rough and rocky terrain, but it also had a crook at the top that could be used to guide the sheep. If a sheep wandered too close to a hole, the shepherd would strike his staff against a rock to warn the straying sheep of danger. If the sheep failed to heed the warning and fell, the shepherd would reach out his staff and loop the crook around the sheep's neck to lift it back to safety. In Psalm 23, David wrote, "Yea, though I walk through the valley of the shadow of death, I will fear no evil: for thou art with me; thy rod and thy staff they comfort me" (v. 4).

Flies were not dangerous like wolves and hyenas, but they constantly irritated the sheep. Those pesky insects would hover around the poor animals' faces and land on their eyes and noses until the only way the sheep could find relief was by rubbing their heads against trees and rocks. This only caused more wounds, which attracted more flies, and the sheep would get caught in a vicious cycle. Relief came only when a caring shepherd would put olive oil on a piece of cloth and dab it against the animals' faces. The oil soothed the self-inflicted wounds and acted as a fly repellant. David may have been alluding to this practice when he wrote of his kind shepherd, "Thou anointest my head with oil" (Psalm 23:5).

Maurine and Scot Proctor have written, "Sheep are helpless creatures, without defenses, unable to protect themselves against roaming wolves or nighttime predators. God gave porcupines quills and cheetahs speed, but sheep he left vulnerable. They are perfect symbols for humanity without the Lord. That is why they need a good shepherd who will stay with them in all kinds of weather. . . . Burned by the sun and parched in the wind, the shepherd's job isn't glamourous or even very picturesque, but the sheep cannot survive without him."[1]

Truly we are helpless without our Savior. Because of the Messiah in a manger, we have a Shepherd who leads us into the fold and makes Himself the gate. He owns us and is not a hireling. We are His, and He knows us by name. He does not run away when danger comes. He protects us with His rod and guides us with His staff. When we fall, He lifts us up and anoints our wounds with oil.

The Good Shepherd Himself asked, "What man of you, having an hundred sheep, if he lose one of them, doth not leave the ninety and nine in the wilderness, and go after that which is lost, until he find it? And when he hath found it, he layeth it on his shoulders, rejoicing" (Luke 15:4–5). Sometimes we relate to the ninety and nine and wonder why Christ would abandon us in search of another. We need to remember the parable was given to the Pharisees who, in their self-righteousness, felt they didn't need a Savior. When I think of the ninety and nine, I don't think of faithful members of the Church. I think of the spirits who followed Satan in the premortal world. Christ did not abandon them. They abandoned

Him. We who chose mortality knew we needed the Savior. We are the ones whom Christ came to rescue. Because of the Messiah in a manger, we have a Good Shepherd who laid our sins and sorrows on His shoulders so we could go home with Him rejoicing.

FEEDING LAMBS

For years, our ward Primary leaders performed the Herculean feat of mounting an annual Nativity production in conjunction with a Christmas dinner. The children of the ward took their turns being Mary, Joseph, shepherds, and wise men. Of course, most were cast as angels and sheep. One year when I was helping out, one of the little girls complained, "I don't want to be a sheep. I want to be Mary."

"Why don't you want to be a sheep?" I asked.

"Because there are so many of them," she responded. "No one will even see me."

"I will see you," I promised.

Don't we all sometimes feel the way that girl felt? With all of God's numberless worlds filled with numberless children, who notices sheep number 32 on stage left?

With all of Christ's followers, how does He care for and love each of us individually?

King Benjamin taught his people, "Believe in God; believe that he is, and that he created all things, both in heaven and in earth; believe that he has all wisdom, and all power, both in heaven and in earth; believe that man doth not comprehend all the things which the Lord can comprehend" (Mosiah 4:9). We can be confident that a God who can create and populate worlds has the power to govern those worlds. God cannot have more children than He can care for.

> *We can be confident that a God who can create and populate worlds has the power to govern those worlds. God cannot have more children than He can care for.*

Similarly, Christ cares for us individually. The inverted five-point stars found on the Nauvoo Temple are symbols of Christ, the "bright and morning star" (Revelation 22:16), reaching down to earth and inviting us to reach up to Him.[2] When Christ was in a crowd and the woman with the issue of blood reached out to touch the hem of His garment, He did not miss it. He knew and turned to her (see Mark 5:24–34). We can be confident that He "reaches our reaching" as well (see *Hymns*, no. 129). After His death and Resurrection in the Holy

Land, Christ visited ancient America. He ministered to people "one by one" (3 Nephi 11:15).

The Savior's love for each individual is demonstrated in His experience with Jairus, who sought Him out and said, "My little daughter lieth at the point of death: I pray thee, come and lay thy hands on her, that she may be healed" (Mark 5:23). The Lord consented to come, but as they neared the house, they were met with the news: "Thy daughter is dead" (v. 35). Jesus said to the grief-stricken father, "Be not afraid, only believe" (v. 36).

When the Lord entered the house, He announced to all who were mourning that the girl was not dead, but only asleep. The scriptures report that "they laughed him to scorn" (v. 40). Nevertheless, Christ took the girl by the hand and said to her in Aramaic, "Talitha cumi." The Bible gives us a translation: "Damsel, I say unto thee, arise" (v. 41). However, in James Hastings's *Dictionary of Christ and the Gospels*, we read that *Talitha* is a transliteration of the Aramaic noun for *lamb*.[3] Just as in English, "lamb" can be a term of endearment for a child. Christ was not calling out to a young girl He did not know. He was calling out to His little lamb, whom He knew and loved dearly. "And straightway the damsel arose, and walked" (v. 42).

Christ cares for all His lambs and lovingly allows us

to engage with Him in caring for each other. President Henry B. Eyring has stated, "The Saints of God have always been under covenant to nourish each other spiritually, especially those tender in the gospel."[4]

> *Christ cares for all His lambs and lovingly allows us to engage with Him in caring for each other.*

If you visit Israel today, you can go to the Church of the Primacy of Peter on the northern shore of the Sea of Galilee. It is a modest Franciscan chapel that commemorates where the risen Lord is said to have come to Peter and the other Apostles and asked them to feed His lambs and sheep.

When I was there, I stood by the water and tried to imagine Jesus and the Apostles eating bread and fish together. I imagined Jesus pointing to the sea, the boat, and the fish cooking on the fire and asking, "Peter, . . . lovest thou me more than these?" In my mind I could almost hear Peter responding, "Yea, Lord; thou knowest that I love thee" and Jesus saying gently, "Feed my lambs" (John 21:15; see also vv. 16–17) and then repeating the injunction two more times.

President Russell M. Nelson has explained that there were two words in the original Greek that were translated as "feed" in English. Two of the times Jesus told Peter to feed His sheep, the word *bosko* was used, which means "to nourish" or "to pasture." The other time the Savior used the term *poi maino*, which means "to shepherd, tend, and protect."[5] It is clear that Christ was asking Peter—and all of us—to nourish, but also to tend and protect His sheep and lambs.

Years ago I was teaching at a session of Especially for Youth at BYU. I finished my final class and was packing up my scriptures and papers when I discovered an anonymous note that had been placed with them: "Dear Brother Wilcox, I am a young woman dealing with a difficult situation in my home. Some things are happening that shouldn't be, and I don't know what to do. I have never had the courage to tell anyone before. I came to EFY fasting and praying for direction. I am going to come to your final class today. Please give me some advice." My heart dropped. This girl had been in the class I had just finished teaching, and I had said nothing. She would not know I hadn't seen the note. Did she feel like I did not think her plea was important enough to address or that I simply didn't care? I felt terrible. Since I would not have another opportunity to address the group, the only thing I could think to do was pass the note along to Brother Jack Marshall, who was the session director that week.

The next day, one of the teachers called in sick, so at

the end of the morning devotional Brother Marshall announced that he would be taking the place of the teacher listed on the program. He then added, "Yesterday, someone left a note for Brother Wilcox that he did not see until his classes were over. He gave the note to me, and I will try to share some advice in this next class, so I hope the author of that note can come."

Not knowing whether or not the girl was even there, Brother Marshall spoke about the cycle of abuse that is sometimes perpetuated in families and how the best way to break it is to say something to Church leaders and legal authorities. "Sometimes we think we will ruin everything, but actually it is the only way that both the abuser and those being abused can get the help they need," Brother Marshall said. As the class ended, he expected the girl to come talk to him, but no one came. Brother Marshall knew that without knowing her name, there was no way he could find her among all the participants. He prayed that if she had been there, she would now find the courage to say something.

On the final night of the session, the youth were to have a dance, which Brother Marshall was going to help chaperone. Before the dance started, a large group of young people gathered around him to say thank you for a great week. One girl said, "Thanks for everything you did for us." As Brother Marshall looked at her, the Spirit indicated to him that she was the one who had written the note. He asked quietly, "You wrote Brother Wilcox the note, didn't you?" The girl was stunned. She had no idea how he knew. Brother Marshall asked, "Would you like to talk?" She nodded, and they pulled away from the group.

She bravely told him about the abuse going on in her home. Brother Marshall listened and testified that God was aware of her situation and loved her. During the course of their conversation she mentioned where she was from. Brother Marshall had recently spoken at a fireside in her home stake and remembered the name of her stake president since he had stayed in his home. When the girl returned to the dance, Brother Marshall found the stake president's phone number, called him, and explained the situation. The stake president said he knew the girl and her family and promised he would meet with her when she came home, get her the help she needed, and notify the proper authorities.

As Brother Marshall and I have reflected on that experience through the years, we have felt humbled to have witnessed such a miracle. We know that the way Brother Marshall identified this young woman was no lucky guess. Similarly, we know that the fact that Brother Marshall had spoken in her stake and knew her stake president was no coincidence. It was one of those amazing times when, as Emily Freeman once said at a Time Out for Women event, "We may not see the finger of the Lord as did the Brother of Jared, but we can certainly see His fingerprints."

The Apostle Paul commanded the elders of the Church, "Take heed therefore unto yourselves, and to all the flock, over the which the Holy Ghost hath made you overseers, to feed the church of God, which he hath purchased with his own blood" (Acts 20:28). That week at EFY, the Holy Ghost prompted some overseers in remarkable ways, and one little lamb was nourished, tended, and protected. The Lord told Peter to feed His sheep, and Peter has told us the same: "Feed the flock of God which is among you. . . . And when the chief Shepherd shall appear, ye shall receive a crown of glory that fadeth not away" (1 Peter 5:2, 4).

Because of the Messiah in a manger, we are never just part of a crowd or congregation. We are individuals. Elder David A. Bednar has written, "The story of Jesus teaching Peter to feed His lambs is not a story about a flock. Rather, it is a story about millions and tens of millions and hundreds of millions of *ones*—because the worth of souls is great in the sight of God."[6] Christ, "the Shepherd and Bishop of [our] souls" (1 Peter 2:25), feeds His sheep.

We "hold a place within his heart" (*Hymns*, no. 187). Impossible? How many times does the Lord have to prove that He can do miracles we cannot comprehend before we remember the Savior's words to Jairus: "Be not afraid, only believe" (Mark 5:36).

At the Primary Nativity production, I spoke to a disappointed little girl who wanted to be cast as Mary so the audience would notice her. Instead, she was one of the sheep. I promised her I would see her, but if I could go back in time, I would say, "Not only will I see you, but *God* will see you, and that's what matters most."

HEARING THE
ANGELS' SONGS

The Tabernacle Choir on steroids!" That is how one Primary child described what it must have been like to hear the angels sing at Christ's birth. Other answers were "Like a rushing waterfall" and "Kind of a cross between classical and modern." Another child just started singing, "Glo-o-o-o-ria in excelsis Deo" straight out of "Angels We Have Heard on High" (*Hymns*, no. 203). We may never know what the angels sounded like or even how long their praises lasted, but we do know the multitude of heavenly hosts performed for a very small audience—a handful of shepherds "abiding in the field, keeping watch over their flock by night" (Luke 2:8). Those who were at home in their beds missed the heavenly music.

I've always believed that some of God's tenderest of tender mercies come to those who are willing to sacrifice a little comfort and convenience to keep watch over His flock. As we serve faithfully in our callings, I'm convinced that sometimes we get to witness miracles and hear angels' songs that others miss.

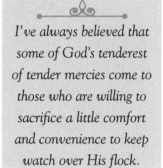

I've always believed that some of God's tenderest of tender mercies come to those who are willing to sacrifice a little comfort and convenience to keep watch over His flock.

I could write about those who serve in bishoprics, Relief Society presidencies, or as ministering brothers and sisters. I could also write about those who sacrifice to lead and teach young people and children or those who serve in temples. However, this story is about two missionaries who have been blessed to hear angels' songs.

In 2007, Bob Evers took an early retirement from working as a supervisor at a cement plant because of a brain tumor. Obviously, the tumor was bad news, but for him early retirement was good news. He is a convert and never served a mission as a young man, so serving together with his wife, Kenalou, was definitely on his bucket list. As soon as Bob's cancer was under control enough for doctors to clear him, he and his wife submitted their mission papers. They were called to serve in Cleveland, Ohio, where they would work in records preservation. Records preservation is the process of preparing and imaging records so they can still be around long after paper copies would disintegrate. It is also the first step in having the records indexed so they can be searched by people worldwide and names can be prepared for the temple.

The Everses learned that people at Church headquarters make arrangements with government, religious, and family history organizations to copy their records. The Church covers the cost and provides the custodians of the records with copies in return for allowing the Church to also keep a copy and make it accessible online. Sometimes records are scanned (at about eighty sheets per minute), and other times they are imaged and digitized (at about six hundred sheets an hour).

When Bob and Kenalou first saw the expensive and complicated cameras and equipment they would be expected to use, they felt overwhelmed. They had to remove all fasteners from the documents, including staples, string, and paper clips; put the documents in labeled folders; focus the camera; make sure each page was surrounded with a black border; and then capture the image. Every week they had to submit their work to Church headquarters, where someone would evaluate it. If it was not up to snuff, they had to do it again. Bob said, "We didn't consider ourselves high-tech people and knew little about computers, but we were willing to learn, and divine help came." If that were not enough, some of the records they encountered were so old they had to moisten the fragile pages so they would not crack or break apart as they were flattened for imaging.

Their trainers assured them they would get the hang of it, and indeed they did. So much so that they had been home from their first mission for only three months when they were called by workers at FamilySearch and asked to do images on a new scanner the Church had just acquired. That turned into another mission in Salt Lake City. Subsequent missions have been to Jerome, Idaho (where they filmed records of Japanese Americans who lived in internment camps during World War II); throughout Utah; Malad, Idaho; Kemmerer, Wyoming; and Globe, Arizona (where they filmed records of the San Carlos Indian Reservation).

Between missions, Bob builds custom cabinets, which helps pay the expenses. Kenalou said, "Each time we signed up for another mission, a cabinet job for an entire house would come through, and that kept us going."

In April of 2017, the Everses got permission to go home from their mission in Arizona to attend the sealing of their son and daughter-in-law on a Friday and the baptisms of their twin grandchildren on Saturday. On Friday evening, Kenalou suffered a heart attack. Thankfully, it did not take her. While Kenalou recovered, Bob took their youngest daughter with him to finish the records they were doing in Arizona. When he got back, the doctor told him and his wife, "I'm afraid your missions are over."

Kenalou replied, "Not over. We'll just have to serve from home for a while."

Bob had already knocked out the wall between two bedrooms in their house and remodeled so there was space for their equipment—a huge scanner that interacts with a computer program to frame images. Now the Everses call it their "mission room," and they continue working. At this point, they have imaged records containing millions and millions of names.

Joseph Smith taught that those who do work in behalf of the departed will one day greet those they have served, at which time those souls will "fall at the feet of those who [have] done their work, kiss their feet, embrace their knees and manifest the most exquisite gratitude."[7] I believe there will be millions of spirits eager to thank Bob and Kenalou in the life to come, but the Everses have received many tender mercies here and now that have seemed like angel songs to them.

For example, Bob said, "We usually have to work so

quickly that we don't have time to notice the names on the records we are imaging. However, one time in Ohio, the Spirit prompted me to slow down and look a little closer at some of the names." Later that day, the employees at the archive were called to attend a meeting in another building. They trusted Bob and Kenalou enough to leave them in charge rather than closing. Not five minutes later, a woman walked into the archive asking for help with her family history. She knew the name of her great-grandfather but needed to find records that might give her more information about him, including the names of his parents and grandparents. She had searched everywhere without success. Bob asked the name and was amazed to hear the exact name he had stopped to notice earlier that day. He said, "I immediately led her to the records she sought. I was the only one who knew where to find the name, because even the archivist would not have thought to look in those records." Bob and Kenalou felt they had witnessed a miracle. They heard a song that only angels could have orchestrated because they were "keeping watch over their flock" (Luke 2:8).

While Bob and Kenalou were serving in Wyoming, they were imaging deed and land records when a man asked whether they might also be interested in imaging naturalization records—documents that were made when people applied for U.S. citizenship. Kenalou said yes, and the man and his assistant brought them over one hundred books. They were moldy and water damaged, very brittle and discolored, but each record contained photographs of the people, names of their parents, and their countries of origin. Kenalou said, "The books were a gold mine. No one at the Church even knew these books existed. If we had not been there at that exact moment, the books may never have been preserved." Once again, the Everses saw the hand of God in the work. They heard the angels' songs they would have otherwise missed.

Similarly, in Vernal, Utah, Bob and Kenalou were working in the office of the county recorder when a man came to research a title. The man's work took him to a miscellaneous file that turned out to contain a census record of Ute Indians. "Hey, check this out," he said to the Everses, who were working nearby. The rare document showed Indian names next to Americanized names and included birthdates and parents' names. Bob and Kenalou would never have looked in the miscellaneous file the man had found, and he would never have mentioned finding the document had the Everses not been there. Imaging that important Native American record was not on their to-do list when they arrived in Vernal, but it ended up being one of the most important things they did there. Again the Everses got to hear the angels' songs because they were engaged in the work.

Bob and Kenalou are the first to admit that such special moments don't happen every day. "Most of the time the work is monotonous and even boring," Bob said, "but every now and then you get reminded of the big picture." Once he imaged a visa that included pictures and names of an entire family that came to the United States from Colombia. Bob wondered where the kids and grandkids of this family might be now. He hoped that some had joined the Church and would one day start searching for their ancestors. "It made me feel good," Bob said, "to think that they could one day look up a copy of the very visa I was holding at that moment and get the information they would need to seal the family in the temple." Bob had always heard returned missionaries tell conversion stories when he was younger. "We don't have those kinds of stories to tell, but we know what we are doing could lead to much fruit down the road."

When Brigham Young was explaining the importance of the work of the Church, he declared, "All the Angels in heaven are looking at this little handful of people."[8] Truly, we are often blessed to hear angelic songs that others don't hear and recognize miracles that others overlook.

Truly, we are often blessed to hear angelic songs that others don't hear and recognize miracles that others overlook.

Because of the Messiah in a manger, angels sang to the shepherds who went "with haste, and found Mary, and Joseph, and the babe" (Luke 2:16). Because of the Messiah in a manger, the shepherds "made known abroad the saying which was told them concerning this child. . . . And the shepherds returned, glorifying and praising God for all the things that they had heard and seen" (vv. 17, 20). Because of the Messiah in a manger, we can do the same.

WISE MEN

RECOGNIZING THE STAR

In Matthew we read of wise men of the East (see Matthew 2:1–12) who followed a star to bring gifts to the child Jesus. The Bible Dictionary explains that these were not scholars or astrologers but spiritually sensitive and knowledgeable "prophets on a divine errand."[1] God led the prophet Lehi and his family to the Americas. Is it not possible that He led other faithful Israelites to other parts of the world? We have the sticks of Judah and Joseph, but we will one day have the sticks of other tribes as well. Wherever the wise men were and whatever tribe they were from, they, like Lehi and Nephi, knew of Christ and were looking forward to His coming.

I once attended a Christmas devotional where Elder Craig A. Cardon of the Seventy spoke. He asked, "How did the wise men know that the star was a sign of Christ's birth?" I assumed it had been prophesied somewhere in the Old Testament, but then Elder Cardon pointed out that our current Old Testament shows no such prophecy. He said, "Every year at Christmastime, people in nearly every Christian denomination celebrate the birth of the Lord by depicting or reenacting the Nativity, complete with wise men following a star. Today we read of 'his star' in the New Testament (Matthew 2:2), but how did the wise men—who didn't have the New Testament—know of the sacred sign?"

Elder Cardon continued, "Most Christians believe there is no scripture or revelation beyond the Bible, yet of the 43 occurrences of the word *star* in the Old Testament, only one has reference to the Savior (see Numbers 24:17), and in that instance the word is a title, not a heavenly object. How did the wise men know to look for a star? People may not realize it, but anyone who believes wise men came at Christ's birth is acknowledging that there had to be other scriptures and revelation in addition to the Bible."

Elder Cardon's insight impacted me deeply. Isn't it fascinating that today all of Christianity speaks and sings of the prophecy of a star that is not found in our current Old Testament but rather in the Book of Mormon? It was Samuel the Lamanite who prophesied, "There shall a new star arise, such an one as ye never have beheld" (Helaman 14:5).

Of course, the wise men couldn't have read of the star in scriptures being recorded in ancient America, but the presence of the prophecy there allows us to assume that similar knowledge could have been revealed to prophets elsewhere. Just as faithful Israelites in America were told to watch for this sign as they awaited the coming of their Savior, surely there were additional groups of faithful believers in other places who were being instructed to look for the same sign.

Isn't it fascinating that today all of Christianity speaks and sings of the prophecy of a star that is not found in our current Old Testament but rather in the Book of Mormon?

The Bible Dictionary states, "It seems likely that [the wise men] were representatives of a branch of the Lord's people somewhere from east of Palestine, who had come, led by the Spirit, to behold the Son of God, and who returned to their people to bear witness that the King Immanuel had indeed been born in the flesh."[2]

Nonbelievers must have also seen the star. They wouldn't have been able to miss such a spectacular sight, but they certainly did not see it as a sign. They merely marveled at the oddity. It was only the wise men who recognized the star for what it was and let it guide them to the Savior. The varied responses are not unlike how people see LDS temples today. Many people see temples as beautiful buildings all lit up at night, but those who are wise see holy beacons that guide them to the Savior.

> *Many people see temples as beautiful buildings all lit up at night, but those who are wise see holy beacons that guide them to the Savior.*

Anciently, the wise men made a long and difficult journey to arrive at their destination. Modern disciples have made similar sacrifices to attend temples. When I was a young missionary in Chile, my companion and I lived with Teobaldo and Maria Llanos and their young daughter, Vicky, in a town named Los Andes. Teo was the president of our small branch. Maria and their eldest daughter, Ana Maria, were the first of their family to be baptized in 1972. Teo was baptized the following year, and then he baptized Vicky. The family was excited when they heard the announcement on March 1, 1975, that a temple was to be built in São Paulo, Brazil—the first temple in South America. Still, they were discouraged that it would be 1,600 miles away. That is about 400 miles farther than the early Saints traveled when they went from Nauvoo to Salt Lake City. Nevertheless, it was closer to the Llanos family than Mesa, Arizona (at the time, the next closest temple), and for that they gave thanks.

When the São Paulo temple was completed in 1978, Teo and Maria were determined to find a way to go. Teo told me later, "Looking back, I can see how the Spirit was working with me overtime. My oldest daughter was married and living in another country, as was our son, who never joined the Church, but I was resolute in my desire to take my wife and youngest daughter to be sealed to me in the temple, along with two other daughters who died as babies."

Maria earned extra money by making empanadas—Chilean meat pies—and selling them to neighbors. She also made clothes and did alterations for people. Teo worked as an accountant and asked for all the overtime he could get. In addition, Teo and Maria sold some of their furniture. By 1979, they were still a little short, so Teo explained the situation to his boss and asked for a loan. The family bought three plane tickets to Brazil.

On the day they went to the temple, Teo recorded the following in his journal: "Today we went to the temple. It was a dream come true. We received our endowments and were married for eternity and sealed to three of our daughters. . . . It was amazing. We were filled with the Spirit. I think our testimonies are stronger now than ever. We return home with our garments to remind us of the covenants we have made." When the family left Brazil the sky was overcast. Teo wrote, "As the plane broke through the clouds we saw the sun shining. Spiritually, we feel like we have broken through the clouds and have seen the light. We leave São Paulo with our hearts full of thankfulness to our Heavenly Father for the privilege to have been in His house and participated in His work there."

Vicky remembers, "The temple workers made our sealing beautiful. They were so sweet and fussed over me as I got ready. I still have the ribbon they put in my hair. I remember the white clothing, the mirrors, and kneeling at the altar with my parents. Most of all, I remember the Spirit." The family stayed near the temple for several days. Vicky, a young teenager at the time, helped in the temple nursery while her parents did session after session.

I lived with the Llanos family the next year, in 1980. In April of that year it was announced that a temple would be built in Santiago, about fifty miles from their home. I asked Teo if he regretted spending the money to go all the way to Brazil now that there would be a temple so close. He responded, "Elder Wilcox, if some Chileans had not sacrificed to go to Brazil, how would God have ever known we loved the temple enough to give us our own?" As the only endowed members in their area, Teo and Maria were instrumental in helping many members prepare to enter the temple. I remember Teo standing before our small branch that met in a rented house and saying with great passion, "Brothers and sisters, the blessings awaiting you in the temple are worth any sacrifice."

Imagine their joy years later as Teo and Maria were also sealed to their oldest daughter and their son, who had passed away by then. They were focused on the temple. Like the wise men of old, the Llanos family recognized the star and followed it to Christ.

Elder Robert E. Wells, emeritus General Authority Seventy, has compared attending the temple to navigating by the stars: "As [Navy] cadets we were taught the science and the practice of this pre-electronic navigation system."[3]

> [He] no longer navigates ships by looking at the stars, but he navigates his life by looking to the temple.

Elder Wells could be in the middle of an ocean with no land in sight, and yet by using the stars he could establish the ship's position and then suggest adjustments in direction so the ship could arrive at the desired destination. Elder Wells no longer navigates ships by looking at the stars, but he navigates his life by looking to the temple. He wrote, "Inside the temple I can establish my position with regard to the ultimate destination of eternal life."[4] Like Elder Wells, we can also go to the temple to determine whether we are on course.

The Llanos family and Elder Wells have been led to Christ by the temple. Others see temples or even attend temples and remain unaffected. When Christ was on the earth, some followed Him, while others did not. Have you ever wondered whether you would have accepted Christ in His day? If you had heard of the miracles surrounding His birth, would you have believed or been skeptical? If you had watched Him grow in Egypt or Nazareth, would you have noticed something special about Him? When He started His ministry, would you have believed and become a disciple, or would you have been apathetic? Would you have listened to His teachings or been too busy milking goats and making cheese to think too much about Him? Would you have sided with those who fought against Him? Elder Wells has told us how we can know exactly where we would have stood then. He wrote, "Our feelings about the temple are the truest indicators of our deepest feelings about Christ."[5]

If we love the temple today, we would have loved Christ in His day. If we seek to go to the temple, we would have sought to be with Christ. If we desire to learn more about the temple, we would have desired to learn more about Christ.

In the meridian of time, the King of kings was born in a manger. Now He has palaces—many temples throughout the world. The wise men came to know the Savior "when they were come into the house"

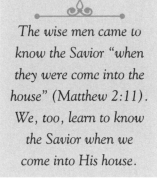

The wise men came to know the Savior "when they were come into the house" (Matthew 2:11). We, too, learn to know the Savior when we come into His house.

(Matthew 2:11). We, too, learn to know the Savior when we come into His house. Because of the Messiah in a manger, we have temples. Within them, we, like Elder Wells, can find direction. We, like the Llanos family, can find salvation and sealing.

Some saw the star of Bethlehem as a novelty and nothing more. Others followed it to Christ. Some see the temples as fancy buildings. Others allow the temple to lead them to the Savior.

ANOTHER WAY

"Where is he that is born King of the Jews?" (Matthew 2:2). That was the question the wise men asked of Herod. The wicked king was troubled by the question. In his pride and arrogance, he probably wanted to respond by saying, "You're looking at him!" Instead, Herod decided to use the wise men's inquiry to his advantage. He "gathered all the chief priests and scribes of the people together, [and] demanded of them where Christ should be born" (v. 4). I can imagine that when the priests relayed the prophecies that Christ would be born in Bethlehem, a false smile crept across Herod's face as he said, "When ye have found him, bring me word again, that I may come and worship him also" (Matthew 2:8).

We don't know how long it took the wise men to locate Jesus and present their gifts. However, we do know that at some point they were "warned of God in a dream that they should not return to Herod," whose heart was hardened and whose motives were evil. Instead, after encountering the Christ, "they departed into their own country *another way*" (Matthew 2:12; emphasis added).

When my son-in-law Landon was serving his mission in Uruguay, he got to call home on Christmas. His father, Larry Laycock, a wise man himself, reminded Landon of what is shared in Matthew 2. He said, "Once the kings found Christ they went home by another route, but it could also mean that they themselves were different. When we encounter Christ, we are meant to be changed. We are meant to return to heaven another way."

One of my students at BYU, Owusu (Woo-Sue) Agyin, is an example of one whose life was changed when he encountered the Savior. His mother is Hawaiian and his father is originally from Ghana. They met and married in southern California. She was a member of the Church, so he joined, but he never took the teachings of the Church to heart. All three of their children were blessed as babies, but the family did not attend church regularly. Most of Owusu's childhood church memories were thanks to his Hawaiian grandmother, who insisted the children attend with her whenever she visited.

When Owusu was seven, his parents divorced and the children lived with their father. That ended any contact with the Church. Each child responded to the divorce in his or her own way. Owusu's older brother fell in with the wrong crowd. His sister withdrew, and Owusu escaped into electronic games.

Four years later, Owusu's dad remarried, and the children decided to move in with their mother. She was not active in the Church at the time, so she was surprised when her fourteen-year-old daughter announced one Sunday that she was going to church. She was doubly surprised when eleven-year-old Owusu said he wanted to go too.

"That was a turning point for me," Owusu said. "I felt like I had come home." Teachers, friends, and leaders surrounded the two young teenagers with support. When the missionaries found out the two had never been baptized, they began visiting and teaching them. Their mom was supportive, but they knew their dad would never give permission for them to be baptized.

Two years went by and a missionary was transferred into their ward who asked questions previous elders had not: "Have you prayed for your father's heart to be softened? Have you fasted about it?" He boldly promised Owusu and his sister that if they would do so, their father would give permission. The two teenagers fasted, prayed, and wrote letters to their father. In January of 2011, he responded. His letter was filled with objections, but at the end he gave his permission. Owusu felt that he had witnessed a miracle. On March 25, 2011, he and his sister were baptized.

Owusu's experience was similar to that of President Howard W. Hunter, whose father also refused to grant permission for his children to be baptized at age eight. It was not until President Hunter and his sister were twelve and ten respectively that they finally convinced their father they were ready. Their faithful examples eventually led to their father's baptism.[6] Owusu's dad has not returned to the Church, but when Owusu's sister decided to serve a mission, it touched her mother's heart. She became active, obtained a temple recommend, and was able to be with her daughter in the temple before she left to serve in Houston, Texas.

Owusu also chose to serve a mission. He was not listening to the October 2012 Saturday conference session in which President Thomas S. Monson announced the lowered age for missionaries. He was at a physical therapy session due to a football injury. His leaders texted him immediately. He started his papers that very day and was called to serve in Mendoza, Argentina.

Owusu loved his mission. He loved the people and the culture. But after he had been out for about eight months, he began to feel weighed down by poor choices he had made when he was younger. "It wasn't anything major," he told me. "It's just that the closer I got to Christ, the more the small things from the past started to pull me down." Owusu finally spoke to his mission president, who counseled him that although he had confessed to his bishop before his mission, perhaps he had not felt godly sorrow as deeply as he should have. His mission president assured him that what he was experiencing was appropriate and healthy. He encouraged Owusu to focus his studies on the Atonement.

As he did, Owusu learned that along with the promise of forgiveness, the grace that flowed from the Atonement also promised development. Christ's gift was not just about coming to peace with the past, but moving forward. "As I learned more about the Atonement, I felt closer to the Savior than ever before," Owusu explained. He saw how his covenant relationship with Christ was affecting his

> *Christ's gift was not just about coming to peace with the past, but moving forward.*

choices and attitude in positive ways. The relationship was more personal than ever before.

Owusu had desperately needed the love and validation his leaders and friends offered when he had first come to church. Those relationships had blessed his life. However, this was different. His relationship with the Savior was changing his life. Owusu said, "Christ had been my anchor during my teenage years. Now He was also becoming my sail." When Owusu completed his mission and came home, he, like the wise men, came home another way.

Because of the Messiah in a manger, we can encounter Him and engage with Him not just once but over and over at every age and every stage. In "The Living Christ" document, we read, "His life, which is central to all human history, neither began in Bethlehem nor concluded on Calvary."[7] His influence was felt in the premortal existence and throughout the Old Testament. The Book of Mormon is evidence that Christianity existed before Christ's birth and will outlast every external and internal attack. Christ's grace was felt during His lifetime and is still felt today. Because of the Messiah in a manger, we can enter a covenant relationship with Him that allows us to experience "more holiness . . . more strivings within, more patience in suff'ring, more sorrow for sin,

more faith . . . joy . . . purpose . . . gratitude . . . purity
. . . [and] strength . . . more freedom from earth-stains,
more longing for home" (*Hymns*, no. 131). Because of
the Messiah in a manger, we, like the wise men, can go
home another way.

BELIEVERS WITHIN THE BOOK OF MORMON AND AT JOSEPH SMITH'S TIME

A GIFT RECEIVED

"Promise you won't get me anything!" Those were the exact words my wife said to me when we were newlyweds. We hardly had enough money to pay bills, so Christmas gifts were a luxury Debi decided we could not afford. These days I am better at speaking the language of "Wife," but back then I thought she really didn't want me to get her anything, so I didn't. Christmas morning came, and Debi was upset.

I tried to explain myself: "But you said . . ."

"Yes," she interrupted, "but at least you could have gotten some small thing or written a note or offered service—some gesture to let me know you care."

It was not my finest moment as a husband. To all the newlywed men who may be reading this: When your wife says the words *promise you won't get me anything*, that means you better get started that very day putting a

gift together or you can kiss your *feliz Navidad* goodbye.
I am not the brightest bulb in the string of Christmas
lights, but I learned my lesson and have tried to be more
thoughtful and considerate since.

We all know it is better to give than to receive,
but, like Debi, we at least want to receive something
from a loved one—anything—to let us know we are not
forgotten. On a much larger
scale, isn't that the message of
Christmas? Christmas is about
giving to others, but it is also
about receiving, for we received
a Savior! No other gift was, is,
or ever will be more important

> Christmas is about giving
> to others, but it is also
> about receiving, for we
> received a Savior!

and meaningful. No other message will ever be so clear:
"God loved us, so he sent his Son, Christ Jesus, the atoning One" (*Hymns*, no. 187). We are not forgotten. We
are valued and loved.

Each December I read the Christmas story from the
Bible, but I also read about the first Christmas in ancient America from the Book of Mormon. About 5 BC
was a period of great instability in the Nephite city of
Zarahemla. People went from being righteous to wicked
in only a few years and continued the plunge downward
with no restraints. The laws that had made the society

great were being disregarded or changed in order to justify every indulgence imaginable. The Gadianton robbers assassinated their opponents and placed themselves on the judgment seats. Most people knew how Nephi, son of Helaman, had brought a famine that had ended war and motivated repentance. They knew he had stood up to corrupt lawyers and revealed the secret plans of Gadianton robbers. But that was about a decade before—old news.

That's when God sent a Lamanite prophet named Samuel to warn the Nephites to repent because Christ's coming was imminent. The people cast Samuel out, but he returned and boldly testified that in five years, Christ would be born. Unbelievers surely scoffed. They must have figured it was pretty easy to prophesy the coming of Christ when it was going to take place across the ocean where it could never be verified by the Nephites. Then Samuel continued and foretold of a day, a night, and a day with no darkness just before the Lord's birth (see Helaman 14:4). This was a sign that the Nephites would be able to verify, but how could the sun go down without bringing darkness? It seemed impossible. Unbelievers threw stones and shot arrows at Samuel, but the Lamanite prophet was protected. He leapt from the wall, returned to his own people, and "was never heard of more among the Nephites" (Helaman 16:8).

Over the next few years, the tension between believers and unbelievers mounted. Believers looked forward to the sign. Unbelievers persecuted and ridiculed. Believers turned to their prophet—Nephi, son of Helaman—who assured them "that the Christ must shortly come" (Helaman 16:4).

Then, just as Romans would one day kill Christians who would not deny, the unbelievers decreed that all believers who did not renounce their faith would be put to death unless Samuel's sign came before a certain day. The faithful turned to their prophet for direction and comfort, but Nephi left. He simply "departed out of the land, and whither he went, no man knoweth" (3 Nephi 1:3). Maybe believers assumed he was translated like Alma the Younger and Moses, but unbelievers probably claimed Nephi ran away—that he knew the sign would never come and he didn't want to die. Samuel never returned, and now Nephi was gone. Unbelievers were surely emboldened by these happenings and, full of hate, they continued to prepare for the coming destruction.

Nephi III, son of Nephi, led in his father's place. On the final day before the believers would be killed, Nephi prayed "mightily to his God in behalf of his people . . .

who were about to be destroyed because of their faith" (3 Nephi 1:11). Imagine his relief when the Lord spoke peace, saying, "On this night shall the sign be given" (3 Nephi 1:13). Nephi must have attempted to spread the news as best he could, but it would have been difficult to reach everyone before that evening.

What was going through the minds of the believers? If they heard Nephi's news, did they believe him? If they had not heard, were they tempted to deny in a last-ditch effort to save themselves and their families? What fears and faith were battling inside them as they looked west to what some may have thought would be their last sunset? What mixture of hope and despair filled their hearts as the sun reached the horizon and began to slip steadily out of sight? Then, suddenly, instead of getting darker and darker, it stayed as light as before.

The impossible had happened. Believers surely wept in joy and vindication. They must have knelt in grateful prayer.

Parents probably gathered children around them and told them to never forget that moment and what it meant: the long-awaited Christ had been born!

Parents probably gathered children around them and told them to never forget that moment and what it meant:

the long-awaited Christ had been born! They had been saved!

When Debi and I were first married, Debi did not want an expensive Christmas gift, but she wanted to know she had not been forgotten. True believers in ancient America wanted the same thing—to know they had not been forgotten. They hoped for some gesture to let them know God was aware of them and cared. The gift they received was amazing. For them, God's love was—literally—as clear as day!

I agree with my friend Michael Wilcox, who has written, "I do not believe that an unlearned farm boy from New York could create such a story. I do not believe any kind of fiction could describe in such simple and undramatic language a moment, a time, a test, a faith, as sublime as the Nephite Christmas story."[1]

Elder David A. Bednar wrote, "The day Jesus was born was a day of deliverance for the believers in the New World. Light as a sign of the Savior's birth literally saved their lives."[2] This was an incredible foreshadowing of what Christ would do for all people. Because of the Messiah in a manger, we are all saved. Because of the Messiah in a manger, we can all know the wonder of receiving the greatest gift ever.

SEEING CHRIST
MORE CLEARLY

A long with remembering the birth of the Savior each December, many Latter-day Saints also remember the birthday of the Prophet Joseph Smith on December 23, 1805. The Smiths were living in Sharon, Vermont, when Joseph was born in a small cabin owned by his grandfather, Solomon Mack. The birth must have made Christmas a happy time for the Smiths and the Macks, but that would not always be the case for Joseph. Consider some difficult Decembers throughout the Prophet's life.

In December of 1823, Joseph mourned the recent and untimely death of his older brother, Alvin. In 1828, Joseph and Emma coped with the loss of their first child and struggled with the disappearance of the 116 pages of the Book of Mormon manuscript. Right on Christmas Day, in 1832, Joseph received a revelation about the

Civil War (see D&C 87). Nothing like contemplating war to dampen the Christmas spirit. The next year found Joseph grieving over the recent expulsion of the Saints from Jackson County.

In 1837, small banks nationwide failed, including the Saints' Kirtland Safety Society. Christmas had to be difficult that year for Joseph as he faced hateful accusations and bitter apostasy. The following December, in 1838, Joseph languished in Liberty Jail. Perhaps one of the hardest Christmases of all came in 1842, when Emma delivered a son who died at birth the day after Christmas.

Of course, there were happy Christmases as well. In December 1835 Joseph wrote in his journal about going sleighing with his children in freshly fallen snow. On December 25 of that year, he penned, "Enjoyed myself at home with my family, all day, it being Christmas." Joseph's last Christmas in 1843 included caroling, visits with friends and family, a delicious dinner, and good music and dancing. The best present that year was when Joseph's friend Orrin Porter Rockwell showed up at his home amid the festivities after having been imprisoned in Missouri for nearly a year.[3]

My wife's ancestors Parshall and Hannah Terry lived in Palmyra, New York, and knew the Prophet Joseph Smith. Their son Jacob was the exact same age as Joseph and was his schoolmate and friend. In 1817, three years before the First Vision, the Terry family moved from New York to Canada and lost contact with the Smiths until 1837, when missionaries taught them. The family was amazed to learn about all that had transpired with the Smith family. The Terrys were baptized the following year and moved to Missouri, anxious to reconnect with their friends the Smiths. Instead, they got there just in time to be expelled from the state because of the extermination order.

In Illinois, the Terrys and Smiths were finally reunited. Parshall and Hannah loved listening to the Prophet preach. They couldn't get over the fact that the boy who had gone to school with their son was now teaching them and thousands of others so powerfully. Like many Saints in their day, the Terrys helped with the construction of the Nauvoo Temple, mourned when Joseph and Hyrum were martyred, faced bitter persecution, and ultimately went west with the Saints in early 1846. But before they left, they received their temple blessings. It was right on December 25, 1845, that Parshall and Hannah received their endowments in the Nauvoo Temple.

Today, many people are quick to label Joseph Smith a fraud, a con man, a false prophet. Others praise his accomplishments. The *Smithsonian* magazine included Joseph Smith in their listing of "the 100 most significant Americans of all time" and in the category of Religious Figures named Joseph Smith as number one.[4] However, the Terrys had an advantage that no one today has. They actually knew Joseph from when he was a child until the end of his life. They not only spoke well of Joseph, but they sacrificed to follow him. Their choices are powerful evidence of Joseph Smith's sincerity and goodness.

All world religions try to help people find God. They all provide a window through which people can attempt to see and understand Him. Some windows are small and clouded by tradition and superstition. Others are larger and clearer. But the window Joseph Smith provided is huge and fully transparent.

Many Christians see Christ through a window framed only by Matthew, Mark, Luke, and John. The window provided by Joseph Smith included the Bible but added the Book of Mormon and other Restoration scriptures, as well as temple teachings and ordinances. Through such an expansive window, we can see Christ more clearly. Brigham Young stated, "Do we differ from others who believe in the Lord Jesus Christ? No, only in believing more."[5]

To me it has always seemed inconsistent that each

December, Christians all over the world celebrate an angel coming to a young girl named Mary (see Luke 1:26–27) and then completely dismiss the possibility of an angel coming to a young boy named Joseph (see JS–H 1:33). In a world where many no longer believe in God, the fact that He sent angels to *both* Mary and Joseph Smith seems like strong evidence that God still believes in us! If God so loved the world that He sent His only begotten Son back then (see John 3:16), then surely He still loves the world enough to send Him again in our day. The Messiah who came to a manger in Bethlehem is the same one who came to a grove in Palmyra and a temple in Kirtland. The Lord who spoke to His servant Paul on the road to Damascus is the same one who spoke to His servant Joseph in Missouri and Nauvoo.

The window provided by Joseph Smith included the Bible but added the Book of Mormon and other Restoration scriptures, as well as temple teachings and ordinances. Through such an expansive window, we can see Christ more clearly.

Was Joseph Smith perfect? No. He never claimed to be. I have heard many criticisms of the Prophet, but few that weren't first leveled against Christ Himself. Two thousand years of criticism have not changed the truth about our Lord, and two hundred years of criticism have not changed the reality of Joseph Smith's divine call. In Doctrine and Covenants we read, "Joseph Smith, the Prophet and Seer of the Lord, has done more, save Jesus only, for the salvation of men in this world, than any other man that ever lived in it" (D&C 135:3). Elder D. Todd Christofferson has further testified, "The Savior has not had among mortals a more faithful witness, a more obedient disciple, a more loyal advocate than Joseph Smith."[6]

> *Two thousand years of criticism have not changed the truth about our Lord, and two hundred years of criticism have not changed the reality of Joseph Smith's divine call.*

Because of the Messiah in a manger, we have a view of eternity. Because of Joseph Smith, we see Christ more clearly. How much richer is our understanding of Jesus, whose birth we celebrate on December 25th, because of Joseph Smith, whose birth we celebrate on December 23rd.

DISCIPLES
IN OUR DAY

PROPHETS PAST, PRESENT, AND FUTURE

The classic tale *A Christmas Carol* was written by Charles Dickens and published in December 1843. In the story, Ebenezer Scrooge's life was changed forever by messages he received from three ghosts: the Ghosts of Christmases Past, Present, and Yet to Come. My life has been similarly changed for the better—not by ghosts but by messages from God through His prophets. Many people acknowledge prophets of the past, but I am thankful to also know we have prophets in the present and will have prophets in the future.

I once tried to explain my faith in prophets to an evangelical Christian friend, who asked, "Is the Mormon Church a Bible-based church?"

I responded, "No, not in the way you are thinking, but yes in a way you may have never considered." She was intrigued by my response, so I continued, "Many

Christians base their faith on the Bible alone. For them, it is their religion."

> Many people acknowledge prophets of the past, but I am thankful to also know we have prophets in the present and will have prophets in the future.

She said, "I would consider myself one of those."

I continued, "But the Bible is not religion. It is a sacred record of people who had religion. We cannot call *them* Bible-based believers, because they did not have the Bible as we have it today. They believed because they had prophets and apostles who were alive, and that is what Latter-day Saints have in addition to the Bible."

I don't think she rushed out to find the missionaries and set a baptismal date, but at least she was willing to listen and understand where I was coming from. People in the Bible did not say, "Turn to John 3:5." The turned directly to John. People in the Bible did not say, "Turn to the epistles of Paul." They turned to Paul. Today, Latter-day Saints consider themselves blessed because we can also turn to living apostles and prophets.[1]

My testimony of living prophets was strengthened many years ago on a plane from California to Utah. It was the weekend right before Christmas. I had been in southern California for several days, speaking to young people at a multistake youth conference. The theme was "Follow the Prophet."

After my last talk, I said goodbye to the group quickly because I simply could not miss my plane. It was almost Christmas and I had to get home to family. Nevertheless, the traffic was terrible and I arrived at the airport too late. "When is the next flight?" I asked an airline worker.

"No more flights," she said mechanically.

"No more flights?" I asked, panicking.

She probably wanted to say, "Isn't that what I just said?" But she restrained herself. After all, it was Christmastime. Automatically, she typed several things into her computer and finally stated, "The last available flight to Salt Lake tonight leaves from a different airport, LAX."

"That's too far away. Isn't there anything closer?"

She checked her computer again, shook her head, and shrugged. There was nothing else. Quickly I rented a car and started toward Los Angeles, all the while singing, "All I want for Christmas is a clear freeway."

I arrived at that huge airport with only minutes to spare. There was no time to check bags—including gifts I had picked up for my kids. I had been away only a few days, but because it was Christmas I was loaded up like a missionary returning after two years.

The uniformed agent was already closing the door when I came panting up to the gate. "Please," I said, hyperventilating, "I've got to get on that plane!"

"But, sir . . ." She started to tell me there was no room in the inn. Then, looking at what must have been a pitiful sight, this kind innkeeper opened the door. Other travelers surely questioned what was causing the delay. When what to their wondering eyes should appear? Brad Wilcox, complete with suitcase and Christmas packages.

I waded between the front few seats and dove for the first empty spot. Once planted, I exhaled loudly. The good man right next to me offered, "May I help you with some of those things?" It was Elder Gene R. Cook, a General Authority Seventy. He smiled, "I'm glad you made it."

"Thanks, Elder Cook," I managed, and he helped me get settled. Once the plane took off, we began to talk.

He asked, "Did you see who you passed at the front of the plane?"

"No, who?"

"The prophet is sitting right up there with his wife."

My first thought was that I had probably just hit him with my luggage. I could see the headlines in the *Church*

News: "Passenger bashes prophet and his wife with Christmas packages." I felt embarrassed.

Elder Cook explained, "He was here for a special regional meeting we just concluded. He is traveling with Elder Boyd K. Packer of the Quorum of the Twelve."

"Really?" I was getting excited. I had just quoted Elder Packer in the talk I had given to the young people. I had just testified of the blessing of following living prophets and apostles. And here I was on a plane with two of them. I love the Brethren. I study their words and try to pattern my life after their examples. Nevertheless, such closeness to them is a rarity for me.

There I was, sitting right beside a humble representative of the Savior. There I was just a few rows behind men I sustained with all my heart as prophets, seers, and revelators—teachers of "known truth," perceivers of "hidden truth," and bearers of "new truth."[2]

The flight attendant offered me a beverage. I didn't want anything. I just pulled out my journal in hopes of recording the special moment I was experiencing. Suddenly, a man interrupted my writing. "Excuse me," said Elder Packer, who now stood next to my aisle seat. Elder Cook moved toward the window, and I stood to let Elder Packer sit down next to him, which also put him right next to me. Elders Cook and Packer talked softly together.

I thought I was writing in my journal the entire time. But looking back at the pages now, I see there is very little there. One would suppose that such a short journal entry could not communicate much. However, this particular entry expresses more than enough to me.

I had just quoted the Apostle who now sat beside me. I had just read Elder Packer's words to the young people: "I have heard his voice and received a witness, even a special witness of him. I pray God that each of us this Christmas will at last open [Christ's] gift and discover who *we* are, and who *he* is."[3]

Elder Packer suddenly turned toward me. "Well, Brad, Elder Cook tells me you have been here addressing the youth."

I nodded.

"What did you tell them?" he asked politely.

"Elder Packer," I spoke quietly, "their theme was 'Follow the Prophet,' so I quoted you. I bore testimony that you are an Apostle—just like Peter, James, and John were Apostles."

Elder Packer sat thoughtfully for a moment. Then, smiling at Elder Cook and back at me, he said, "If you're going to go running around saying things like that, I guess I need to try to do a little better."

We spoke for several more minutes, and then Elder Packer returned to his seat. I looked across the now-empty chair between us and caught Elder Cook's eyes.

"Thank you for saying something to him."

Elder Cook raised his eyebrows as if to say, "Who, me?"

"Yes, you," I said. I knew that Elder Cook had to have whispered something to Elder Packer about the crazy guy beside him named Brad who was excited to be so close to him. Elder Cook had provided a treasured moment for me.[4]

> *In a world where, in too many cases, Christ is seen as nothing more than a statue in a manger scene, I appreciate those who stand as His authorized servants and testify that He lives and leads us today.*

In a world where, in too many cases, Christ is seen as nothing more than a statue in a manger scene, I appreciate those who stand as His authorized servants and testify that He lives and leads us today. Jesus is no longer a baby. He is fully grown and directs us as He always has, through the words of prophets and apostles in our day. In 1974, President Thomas S. Monson testified that as we come to know Christ, "We discover he is more than the babe in Bethlehem, more than the carpenter's son, more than the greatest teacher ever to live. We come to know him as the Son of God. . . . He lives. . . . I so testify."[5] Such words give me security and peace. Such a testimony gives me evidence for my faith.

On a visit to Israel I listened to a Jewish rabbi bemoan the fact that Judaism has so many different branches and movements. He said, "If only we had a living prophet to clarify God's will!" I thought, *Hey, we've got one of those!* Similarly, at an interfaith symposium at BYU, I heard an evangelical Christian leader bemoan the fact that the Bible is interpreted so differently by various Christian denominations. He said, "If only we had a prophet today who could tell us which is the correct interpretation!" Again I thought, *Hey, we've got one of those!*

President Harold B. Lee once wrote, "That person is not truly converted until he sees the power of God resting upon the leaders of this church, and until it goes down into his heart like fire."[6] I have felt that fire many times.

Three ghosts came to Scrooge—the Ghosts of Christmas Past, Christmas Present, and Christmas Yet to Come. They helped him see clearly and change his life. Because of the Messiah in a manger, we have prophets. In the past, present, and future, we have special messengers who help us see clearly and make positive changes.

LET'S GET
CHRISTMASING!

Recently while walking through a crowded airport, I saw a large ad showing a picture of a woman leisurely sleeping above the words: "Let's get Sundaying." I love sleeping in as much as the next person, but the ad made me realize—once again—that Latter-day Saints don't Sunday like the lady in the picture. For many of us, Sunday is one of the busiest days of the week. We call it the Lord's day and strive to make it a delight by serving Him and each other.

Similarly, disciples of Christ don't Christmas like others either. For us it is not about office parties with open bars and cruise ships with casinos. It's not about end-of-the-year charitable donations to get tax breaks. For us, Christmasing includes a lot of good, old-fashioned, sincere, selfless service.

Most bishops have stories to share of people passing

them extra cash at Christmas to give to those in need or ward members anonymously dropping off food and gifts for their neighbors. One bishop told me of a single mom who scheduled an appointment to see him. Considering her difficult financial situation, he assumed she would ask for a little assistance. Instead she brought her children, and they asked if he knew of a needy family in the ward that they might be able to help for Christmas.

I recall serving as the bishop of a young single adult ward whose members were determined to take on a sub-for-Santa project. I worried because I knew most of these YSAs were working minimum-wage jobs to pay rent and tuition. Despite my concerns, the ward council convinced me that if everyone in the ward gave a little, then together we could pull it off.

They planned an auction to raise the needed funds. One girl offered an apartment cleaning to the highest bidder. A recently returned missionary who had served in Japan auctioned off a Japanese meal. Our family sold a candlelight dinner at our home complete with my youngest children acting as waiters. The ward members ended up helping a family in need, but they also ended up serving each other along the way.

Some accuse Latter-day Saints of engaging in service in an attempt to work or earn our way to heaven.

However, Latter-day Saints do not serve others because we trust more in works than in faith. Our service is a natural and inevitable outgrowth of our faith. We don't do sub-for-Santa projects because we are earning God's grace, but because we are returning grace for grace and emulating our Savior.

> *Latter-day Saints do not serve others because we trust more in works than in faith. Our service is a natural and inevitable outgrowth of our faith.*

I recall another Christmas, which I spent in prison. No, I wasn't *in* prison, but I had been asked to speak at the Utah State Prison by Chuck Thompson, who was serving as an LDS bishop there. When Bishop Thompson called to get some information that he needed to complete the required paperwork for me to enter the prison, he also asked whether I would be willing to come a few hours early and visit one-on-one with some of the inmates in maximum security. "They are not permitted to attend the meeting where you'll speak," he explained. Of course I agreed.

When the day of the visits came, I met with Bishop Thompson and we entered the prison together. Before we entered maximum security, he said, "Brad, these men have made horrible choices and are dealing with serious consequences. Nevertheless, some of them have found the Savior's love in prison."

I spoke with one man on death row. He said, "I'm on a journey of forgiveness—seeking forgiveness from those I hurt and from the Lord. I am also seeking the Lord's help as I try desperately to forgive myself." When Bishop Thompson and I left this man, the bishop told me how the inmate had watched a documentary about leprosy in India and wanted to help. He became involved with Rising Star Outreach, an organization started by Becky Douglas, an LDS woman seeking to lift those affected by leprosy. The inmate wanted to contribute. Even though his job in the prison paid only pennies an hour—enough to buy a soda now and then—he gave up his sodas and sent the little bit he saved each month to help with the charity. His example inspired other inmates to donate as well.

I met another man whose feet and arms were chained to a table across from where I sat. He spoke of regrets in his life and the challenges he faced. "I no longer am a member of the Church in full fellowship, but I know with all my heart that it is true. I'm trying my best to be a light to others while I'm here." When we left him, Bishop Thompson told me how this inmate had encouraged others in maximum security to watch general conference with him by organizing a general conference bingo game. He created cards filled with words that might be said in the talks and let the men claim squares when they heard the words. He actually motivated these hardened prisoners to listen to the speakers the same way parents often motivate their children.

Yet another inmate told me of the thousands of names he had indexed and how grateful he was to be able to help with family history work. He was not just counting down the days until his release. He was making those days count. All the men I met were. Whether it was contributing to charities, playing general conference bingo, or doing family history, I was amazed at how these men were finding ways to serve despite their circumstances.

Of course, there were others in the prison who didn't want anything to do with the bishop and me in our white shirts and ties, but even they were respectful. They knew Bishop Thompson and admired him for the good he was doing. When the bishop and I parted ways at the end of the evening, I thanked him for his service. He responded, "You need to understand that I am not helping these inmates as much as they are helping me."

Bishop Thompson then confided that he had struggled with chemical depression throughout his life. Living in "darkness at noonday" is how he described the experience. He continued, "I'm not talking about getting discouraged about a bad grade or being down after getting a traffic ticket. I am talking about when your emotional elevator plummets to the basement and you can't snap out of it." He shared experiences of times when all he wanted to do was sleep or lie in bed. "But the more I did nothing, the worse I felt."

Bishop Thompson said that when he was younger, his father would say, "Why do you get down? You have so much going for yourself and your family." The bishop knew his dad was right, but his dad's words only made him feel worse.

Bishop Thompson eventually sought professional help and was prescribed medication. "However," he continued, "even with the medication, I have learned that the only thing that breaks the cycle for me is service." Sometimes it was writing letters or thank-you notes. Other times he would put himself in charge of remembering birthdays of family and ward members. "Service is my therapy. It's the only thing that gets my emotional elevator out of the basement."

When I left the prison that day, I felt full of the Christmas spirit. I loved the service that I had been involved in and the service I had observed. I loved the perspective Bishop Thompson shared and asked him to stay in touch and give me updates on some of the inmates.

A while later, he wrote to let me know that after five years, he had been released from serving in the prison. He also gave me the bad news that doctors had found two tumors in his brain—one that was inoperable. Biopsies showed they were both cancerous, stage four. He wrote, "I used to minister to men at the prison who had death sentences. Now I know how they feel."

I worried about what this news would do to a man who had told me privately how precarious his emotional health was at times. Would this send his elevator to the basement never to come up again? My concerns were unfounded. I underestimated the power of years and years of choosing service. It was now a habit. Despite the diagnosis, this good man continued to reach out to others in Christlike service. He said, "If you think about it, Christ had a death sentence too, but He didn't let it stop Him from serving."

> I underestimated the power of years and years of choosing service. It was now a habit.

Bishop Thompson asked each morning for Heavenly Father to guide him to someone needing a little help or encouragement. Once he was guided to assist a young lady trying to change a tire at the side of the road. Bishop Thompson helped her. Another time he saw a young father attempting unsuccessfully to put gas in his car at the side of the freeway. Bishop Thompson stopped, made a funnel out of a piece of paper, filled the tank, and sent the grateful father and his family on their way. Sometimes he was guided to someone who simply needed a compliment or kind word. Other times he was prompted to learn and remember someone's name. Sometimes he just offered a hug to a friend or family member.

Despite the bleakness of his diagnosis, he chose to stay positive and handle awkward moments with humor. When his head was shaved for surgery, he went to work and told everyone he had tried a new barber but didn't recommend him. When a ward member brought by a loaf of homemade bread to express sympathy, he shocked her by jokingly saying, "I'm really offended that you didn't bring it when it was still warm." He and his visitor couldn't stop laughing.

In his last email to me before he passed away, Bishop Thompson wrote, "In everyone's life there is a final chapter. We all will die someday. Some chapters end suddenly. Others take longer. I have had the good fortune to have had a couple of final years with my wife and family. Every morning when I wake up I say, 'We have another day.' My wife Jeanne says, 'We'll take it!' I'm grateful I have had this time. I have done my best to have a good attitude, serve others, and learn to be a good finisher. I bring to God my broken heart and contrite spirit, and with my faith and testimony intact, I do not ride off into the sunset, but into a sunrise."

Because of the Messiah in a manger, we have the greatest example of someone who turned outward in service even in the most difficult circumstances. We can follow the example of our Lord and serve. Let's get Sundaying! Let's get Christmasing!

LOVE MATTERS

Before I began teaching at BYU, I taught sixth grade in Provo. Those years of teaching have provided me with wonderful friends and great memories. One of those memories happened at Christmastime with a boy named James.

"Let's get started," I said to my class one December morning. "I need to get the roll turned in. Is there anyone missing today?"

"James," several of the students responded in unison.

I glanced at the boy's empty seat while marking the roll. I might have felt a little relieved that he was gone, since James was a boy who ran at a pace that would leave a bullet train in the dust. He was sensitive, happy, handsome, and sociable—extremely sociable. I might have been relieved that the seat was empty, except that I enjoyed James so much. He had the personality of all of

Santa's elves put together and more sparkle than holiday punch with 7UP in it. James had more questions than most, more alibis than many, and two shining eyes that would win hands down over Rudolph's nose in any brightness competition. I was sorry he was absent.

The class finished reading and P.E. We were starting math when, to my surprise, James straggled in. "Hello, there," I greeted him. "I was afraid you wouldn't be here today."

He dumped a folded note in my hand and slumped toward his desk. I opened the paper and began to tease by saying aloud as if I were really reading, "Please excuse James for being late. He wasn't even going to come but he couldn't stand the thought of missing school lunch." The students all groaned at my bad joke while I read the real words silently to myself: "Dear Mr. Wilcox, James has been at the doctor again—more problems with his heart. It looks like there will be another surgery at Primary Children's Hospital soon."

I didn't feel like joking anymore. I began the math lesson, but it was as if I were suddenly switched to autopilot. My mouth was moving, my fingers held a marker, I was even writing problems on the board, but my mind was somewhere else. My thoughts were on James.

"Mr. Wilcox," one of the girls called, raising her

hand, "seven times seven is not twenty-one." Like turning the knob on a radio, I tuned back into the problem I was solving with the class.

"Well, you're right about that," I laughed. "Let's try this problem again." Several examples later, I divided the children into small groups with some problems to work on together. I watched James drag through the transition. He moved his chair to be with the others but never lifted his eyes from the desktop. That morning I had marked on the roll that James was absent. Later I had changed it, but now I didn't know what to think. There was a body in a chair, but it was not my usual James.

When the bell rang at the end of the day, I called James back and asked to speak with him. As we waited for a few straggling students to leave, I asked James to help me put up a chart of the next day's schedule. When we were finally alone, I turned to my quiet helper. "What's up?" I asked.

He still didn't lift his gaze. "The valve in my heart isn't working again."

"So what's going to happen?" I walked to my big overstuffed reading chair, sat down, and motioned for James to come closer.

"They're going to have to do another open-heart surgery." James had already been through that experience when he was in the first grade. At the start of the year, his parents had explained the situation to me so I would know that there were some activities in which James had to be careful.

"I thought this was all behind you," I said softly.

"So did I," he sighed.

"What are they going to do?"

"First, they will cut into my chest, and then they will open up my heart, and then they will take out the valve that doesn't work and put in a pig valve."

"How do you feel about that?"

"I think it's gross! I don't want a pig valve. I think that's sick. I want a bionic valve."

His comment made me smile. Obviously he had been watching reruns of *The Six Million Dollar Man* on TV. I asked, "What happens if the pig valve doesn't work?"

"I guess they'll just take it out and put in another one."

"What happens if that one doesn't work?" By asking again I wasn't trying to be insensitive. I sincerely wanted to know the backup plan.

"Then," James said matter-of-factly, "I guess I'll just die."

That was not the backup plan I wanted. The classroom was silent. Neither James nor I spoke. I looked into the eyes of my young student and said, "Don't die, James. You can have my heart."

"No, Mr. Wilcox," he smiled—the first smile I'd seen all day. "I can't take your heart. You have a good heart. I love your heart." I had wanted to lift James. I had wanted to help and love him. But, like the true child he was, he lifted me. He helped me. He loved me.

I don't remember whether the snow had already been falling throughout the afternoon or if it began then. All I remember are the unusually heavy flakes that came down outside my classroom window covering the playground with a blanket of snow—a frozen, icy blanket that, considering the moment, looked strangely warm and comforting to me.[7]

James made it through that year and several surgeries since. In fact, last time I saw him, this boy who used to come to my waist was taller than I am. He and his wife, Paige, just celebrated twenty years of marriage and have four great kids. I'm proud of the good choices James has made and all he has become, but no matter how many years pass, I will always remember him as the young boy in my sixth-grade class.

Jesus said, "Suffer little children to come unto me, and forbid them not: for of such is the kingdom of God" (Luke 18:16). After His Crucifixion and Resurrection, that same Jesus stood in the Americas and took the children, "one by one, and blessed them, and prayed unto the Father for them" (3 Nephi 17:21). The Savior loves His little ones. Perhaps this is why those who have the wonderful opportunity of working with little ones feel a special closeness to the Savior as they celebrate His birth.

The Savior loves His little ones. Perhaps this is why those who have the wonderful opportunity of working with little ones feel a special closeness to the Savior as they celebrate His birth.

When Elder Jeffrey R. Holland was president of BYU, he wrote a Christmas message to the students and faculty at the end of the semester: "I wish for you some contact with a child . . . [to see] the awe and wonder and wide-eyed delight with which a child greets Christmas—and Christ."[8]

That wish comes true for me every year. And because of my contact with children in schools, Primary, and in my family, Christmas is more than gift-wrapped boxes, songs about holly berries, and home-baked goodies. For me, Christmas is love—the pure love of Jesus Christ, of children, and a sixth-grade boy named James.

We live in a world where "hate is strong and mocks the song of peace on earth, good will to men" (*Hymns,* no. 214). The Internet informs us so quickly and thoroughly of all society's ills that we feel we have no choice but to surrender to the negativity and incivility that surrounds us. We feel that joining in the road rage, divisiveness, and bullying is our only defense. But, deep down, we know there is another way. "A new commandment I give unto you," said Jesus, "That ye love one another; as I have loved you" (John 13:34).

"Silent Night" may be the most beloved of all Christmas carols. In all the times I've sung it, only recently did I notice the placement of an apostrophe that changed the entire meaning of the third verse for me: "Silent night! Holy night! Son of God, love's pure light" (*Hymns*, no. 204). I had always sung the words thinking that the Son of God loves pure light, which is true. However, when I looked at the words written out, I realized that Joseph Mohr, who wrote the text, was not just communicating that Christ loves pure light. He was saying that the Son of God *is* love's pure light. Christ is the light of love. We don't need to fight fire with fire. We can fight fire with love. "God is not dead, nor doth he sleep; The wrong shall fail, the right prevail" (*Hymns*, no. 214).

Because of the Messiah in a manger, love matters. Acting and not reacting, turning the other cheek, going the extra mile, and forgiving others matter. Because of the Messiah in a manger, such choices are possible. We can love others, because "He first loved us" (1 John 4:19). Our prideful and unrepentant selves can be subdued because of His sacrifice. "Greater love hath no man than this, that a man lay down his life for his friends" (John 15:13). Because of the Messiah in a manger, people matter. Kindness and respect matter. Love matters.

CONCLUSION

My mom, Val C. Wilcox, loved to write poetry and lyrics. Many of her lyrics were put to music by her dear friend Janice Kapp Perry. One song that our family sings every Christmas is called, "That Night in the Stable." I've included the music (see page 135) so you can sing along:

> *That night in the stable it must have been cold there*
> *So I would have held Him and warmed baby Jesus—*
> *Warmed baby Jesus as He has warmed me.*
> *That night in the stable it must have been bright there*
> *With Bethlehem's starlight around baby Jesus—*
> *Brightening Jesus as He brightens me.*
> *That night in the stable it must have been peaceful*
> *As Mary so lovingly held baby Jesus—*
> *Loving Lord Jesus as He has loved me.*

In the lyrics of the song I hear my mom's testimony: Jesus warmed her, brightened her, and loved her. He does the same for all of us. Mom once told me how having me right on Christmas Day forever changed the way she thought of Mary, Joseph, and the baby Jesus. She explained, "I had always thought of Mary as the beautifully dressed, serene figure we see in manger scenes, but, Brad, your birth blew that image to pieces for me!"

Because Mom went into labor on December 24th and delivered me on the 25th, she knew Mary had had painful contractions. She knew that whatever Mary had worn was certainly not clean and beautiful. It surely was stained.[1] Mom said, "I was in a sterile hospital delivery room. She was probably in a cave that served as a stable for animals. It surely smelled. I was blessed to have the help of experienced doctors and nurses. Mary had Joseph, who loved her, but who was probably unprepared to deliver a baby. Nevertheless, I'm sure he did the best he could."

Elder Jeffrey R. Holland once wrote, "I wonder what emotions Joseph might have had as he cleared away the dung and debris. I wonder if he felt the sting of tears as he hurriedly tried to find the cleanest straw and hold the animals back. I wonder if he wondered: 'Could there be a more unhealthy, a more disease-ridden, a more despicable circumstance in which a child could be born?'"[2]

My birth on Christmas provided my mom with insights about Mary and Joseph, but it also gave her a different view of Jesus. Mom recalled that her greatest realization of all was that Jesus must have cried like I did. Mom said, "I found out the song is wrong." She was referring to the Christmas carol "Away in a Manger" in which we sing, "But little Lord Jesus, no crying he makes" (*Hymns*, no. 206). My mom used to say, "We don't even know who wrote those lyrics. The hymnbook says, 'Anonymous.' Well, Anonymous must have never been around a real baby!"

Perhaps some people are put off by the thought of a crying baby Jesus, but to me the image is beautiful. From His first breath and His first cries, He would know what it is to be fully human, just as He knows what it is to be fully divine. At Christmas we celebrate the birth of a *real* baby to a *real* mother and a *real* Heavenly Father. We received a *real* Savior who performed a *real*

At Christmas we celebrate the birth of a real baby to a real mother and a real Heavenly Father. We received a real Savior who performed a real Atonement, without which we would have all been really lost.

133

Atonement, without which we would have all been *really* lost.

Because of the Messiah in a manger, we have access to light, grace, immortality, eternal life. We can know God and Christ, our Good Shepherd. Our love for Them expands because of temples, the Book of Mormon, and Joseph Smith. Because of the Messiah in a manger, we can look to living prophets, enjoy lives of service, and feel the *real* difference Christ's pure love can make at Christmastime and always.

That Night in the Stable

Words by:
Val Camenish Wilcox

Music by:
Janice Kapp Perry

NOTES

INTRODUCTION

1. "Joy and Spiritual Survival," *Ensign*, November 2016, 82.

CHRIST AND HIS GIFTS

1. *I Know That My Redeemer Lives: Latter-day Prophets Testify of the Savior* (Salt Lake City: Deseret Book, 1990), 77.

2. "Hungering and Thirsting after Righteousness," in *The Sacrament* (American Fork, UT: Covenant Communications, 2010), 78–79.

3. See Tomie dePaola, *The Legend of the Poinsettia* (New York: G. P. Putnam's Sons, 1994).

4. "In Him All Things Hold Together," BYU devotional, May 31, 1991, https://speeches.byu.edu.

5. "The Living Bread Which Came Down from Heaven," *Ensign*, November 2017, 37.

6. "The Living Bread Which Came Down from Heaven," 38–39.

7. John A. Widtsoe, "Symbolism in the Temples," in Archibald F. Bennett, ed., *Saviors on Mount Zion: Course no. 21 for the Sunday Schools* (Salt Lake City: The Church of Jesus Christ of Latter-day Saints, 1950), 168.

HOLY FAMILY

1. New York: Scholastic, 1995.

2. "Behold Thy Mother," *Ensign*, November 2015, 48.

3. Joseph Smith, in *The Joseph Smith Papers*, History 1838–1856, vol. C-1, 2 November 1838–31 July 1842, available online at http://www.josephsmithpapers.org.

4. "Maybe Christmas Doesn't Come from a Store," *Ensign*, December 1977, 65.

5. See "What on Earth Are Swaddling Clothes?" in *New Testament Commentary*, Brigham Young University, 2014, https://www.byunewtestamentcommentary.com/what-on -earth-are-swaddling-clothes/.

6. "What on Earth Are Swaddling Clothes?" in *New Testament Commentary*.

7. See *When Heaven Feels Distant* (Salt Lake City: Deseret Book, 2018), 74–75.

8. "Swallowed Up in the Will of the Father," *Ensign*, November 1995, 22–23.

9. Special thanks to Cori Connors and her alternate verse to "The First Noel," shared on her album *One Small Boy* (Steven Roses Music, 2010).

10. See Katarina Jambresic, *A Global Testimony* (New York: Katarina Jambresic, 2014), 386.

11. *A Global Testimony*, 387.

12. Joseph Smith, in *The Joseph Smith Papers*, History 1838–1856, vol. E-1, 1 July 1843–30 April 1844, available online at http://www.josephsmithpapers.org.

13. "The Grandeur of God," *Ensign*, November 2003, 70.

14. "Young Women Theme," available online at https:///www .lds.org/young-women/personal-progress/young-women -theme?lang=eng.

SHEPHERDS AND ANGELS

1. "Were You There?" in *Keeping Christmas* (Salt Lake City: Deseret Book, 1996), 107.

2. Truman G. Madsen, personal communication to author, June 2002.

3. James Hastings, *A Dictionary of Christ and the Gospels* (New York: Charles Scribner's Sons, 1908), 2:697.

4. "Feed My Lambs," *Ensign*, November 1997, 82.

5. See "Shepherds, Lambs, and Home Teachers," *Ensign*, August 1994, 16.

6. *One by One* (Salt Lake City: Deseret Book, 2017), 66; emphasis in original.

7. Horace Cummings, as quoted in Truman G. Madsen, *Joseph Smith the Prophet* (Salt Lake City: Bookcraft, 1989), 99.

8. As quoted in Michael De Groote and Ronald L. Fox, *Visions of Freedom* (American Fork, UT: Covenant Communications, 2015), 16.

WISE MEN

1. Bible Dictionary, "Wise Men of the East," 789.

2. Bible Dictionary, "Magi," 727–28.

3. *Hasten My Work* (Salt Lake City: Bookcraft, 1996), 90.

4. *Hasten My Work*, 90.

5. *Hasten My Work*, 85.

6. See Eleanor Knowles, *Howard W. Hunter* (Salt Lake City: Deseret Book, 1994), 38.

7. "The Living Christ: The Testimony of the Apostles," *Ensign*, April 2000, 2.

BELIEVERS WITHIN THE BOOK OF MORMON AND AT JOSEPH SMITH'S TIME

1. "The True Spirit of Christmas," in *A Celebration of Christmas* (Salt Lake City: Deseret Book, 1988), 9.

2. *One by One* (Salt Lake City: Deseret Book, 2017), 77.

3. See Larry C. Porter, "Christmas with the Prophet Joseph," *Ensign,* December 1978, 9–11.

4. R. Scott Lloyd, "Joseph Smith atop Smithsonian Magazine's Top Religious Figures List," *Church News,* January 13, 2015, https://www.lds.org/church/news/joseph-smith-atop -smithsonian-magazines-top-religious-figures-list?lang=eng.

5. *Journal of Discourses,* 26 vols. (Liverpool: Latter-day Saints' Book Depot, 1854–86), 13:56.

6. "The Atonement and the Resurrection," *Religious Educator,* vol. 7, no. 1 (2006), 11.

DISCIPLES IN OUR DAY

1. See Joseph Fielding McConkie, *Here We Stand* (Salt Lake City: Deseret Book, 1995), 41–43.

2. See John A. Widtsoe, *Evidences and Reconciliations,* comp. G. Homer Durham (Salt Lake City: Bookcraft, 1960), 256–59.

3. Boyd K. Packer, *A Christmas Parable* (Salt Lake City: Bookcraft, 1986), 13; emphasis in original.

4. This experience was originally shared in Brad Wilcox, "Beneath My Birthday Tree," in *A Christmas to Remember* (Salt Lake City: Deseret Book, 1990), 19–23.

5. "The Paths Jesus Walked," *Ensign,* May 1974, 49–50.

6. "The Strength of the Priesthood," *Ensign,* July 1972, 103.

7. This experience was originally published in Brad Wilcox, "A Teacher's Christmas," in *The Magic of Christmas* (Salt Lake City: Deseret Book, 1992), 86–89.

8. *The Daily Universe,* vol. 37, no. 67 (December 12, 1983), back cover.

CONCLUSION

1. This idea is also beautifully communicated in the song "Real" on Mercy River's Christmas album *All Is Bright.* The music

and lyrics are by Chris Stevens and Nichole Nordeman, Birdwing Music, 2013.

2. "Maybe Christmas Doesn't Come from a Store," *Ensign*, December 1977, 65.

IMAGE CREDITS

Border: Vector/Shutterstock.com

Background: Attitude/Shutterstock.com

Poinsettia, page 1: Naddya/Shutterstock.com

Nativity, page 25: Adyna/Getty Images

Bells, page 45: Happy Icons/Shutterstock.com

Star, page 71: Shafran/Shutterstock.com

Gift box, page 89: losw/Shutterstock.com

Candle, page 103: LynxVector/Shutterstock.com

ABOUT THE AUTHOR

Brad Wilcox is an associate professor in the Department of Ancient Scripture at Brigham Young University, where he also enjoys teaching at Campus Education Week and Especially for Youth. He speaks at Time Out for Women events and is the author of *The Continuous Atonement*, *The Continuous Conversion*, *The 7-Day Christian*, and the BYU devotional "His Grace Is Sufficient." In 2018, his book *Changed through His Grace* received the Harvey B. and Susan Easton Black Outstanding Publication award for LDS scholarship. As a young man, Brad served his mission in Chile, and in 2003 he returned to that country to preside over the Chile Santiago East Mission for three years. He also served as a member of the Sunday School general board from 2009 to 2014. Brad and his wife, Debi, have four children and eight grandchildren.